DUELING
IN
CHARLESTON

Plein Air Pride by Jackie Roche, 2012, oil on canvas. An award-winning Charlotte artist, Roche began painting in 1968 after travels through Europe. Her work has been featured in various exhibitions around the Southeast. She is a past president of the Mint Museum Auxiliary and former vice-president of its board of trustees. *Private collection, photo by Sean Money.*

DUELING

IN

CHARLESTON

VIOLENCE REFINED IN THE
HOLY CITY

J. GRAHAME LONG

Charleston ┃━┃ London
THE
History
PRESS

Published by The History Press
Charleston, SC 29403
www.historypress.net

Copyright © 2012 by J. Grahame Long
All rights reserved

First published 2012

Manufactured in the United States

ISBN 978.1.60949.503.9

Library of Congress CIP data applied for.

For Lissa

CONTENTS

ACKNOWLEDGEMENTS

I wish to express my tremendous thanks to the following for their help and support:

Jackie Roche and family for their lifelong support and compassion for my family and for me; Frank Justice for allowing me to interrupt his well-earned retirement; Kincheloe for her unexpected but most appreciated watercolor; Ashley Heslop, "my lawyer"; Paul Matheny, chief curator of art, South Carolina State Museum; Mary Jo Fairchild, archivist, South Carolina Historical Society; Libby Wilder, librarian, *Post and Courier*; Mark Murray-Flutter, senior curator of firearms, Royal Armouries; Bridget O'Brien, museums coordinator, Historic Charleston Foundation; Dr. Howard Kurtzman, MD, Hugh C. Lane Jr., Laurens Smith, Charlie Rose, Carol Ann Dummond and DeCody Marble for their additional research, input and photos; and Adam Ferrell, publishing director, and Hilary Parrish, editorial department manager, The History Press.

Thanks as well for the unfailing support of the Charleston Museum staff, especially executive director John Brumgardt and assistant director Carl Borick for their research and guidance; archivists Jennifer Scheetz and Jennifer McCormack for providing much-needed research materials (sometimes at a moment's notice); exhibits tech and graphic designer Sean Money for his design wizardry and photographic talent; and, of course, assistant curator of history Neil Nohrden, my right arm in the history department (not to mention left arm, both legs, feet, eyes and ears).

Finally, thanks to my loving wife and daughters for their encouragement throughout this work and to my parents, who long ago drove me up and down the eastern seaboard to all those museums and historic sites—it was worth it.

Chapter I

SINNERS IN THE HOLY CITY

Charleston's Hot Weather, Hotter Tempers

O ver the years it has been argued by historians, professors, even myriad
tour guides that South Carolinians—Charlestonians especially—
participated in more duels than any other group of people in the nation,
quite possibly the entire North American continent. This domestic opinion
is subjective, of course, but hardly comes as a surprise to many natives whose
forebears were part of the richest and fastest-growing city in British North
America. Practiced from the colonial period and well through the nineteenth
century, dueling was an inherently dangerous means of settling disputes and
resting arguments. Though certainly not restricted to South Carolina, it
seemed to find full expression here in both frequency and public acceptance.

By the late 1700s, the diversity of European colonists in the Carolina
Lowcountry region was remarkable. By 1780, there were nine separate
ethnic groups cohabitating in a city already more than a century old, and
each one of them carried their own distinct talents, trades and traditions
from their respective homelands.[1]

Among these jumbled creeds, Charleston was conspicuous for its seemingly
endless supply of hot-tempered duelists and their wanton, albeit elegant
armed conflicts. Even today, just a cursory database search through any
of the city's newspapers will return a hefty number of results. Newspapers
and periodicals regularly announced the outcomes of concluding duels, not
unlike modern-day sports pages. From August 1808: "It is reported and we
fear too much truth, that a duel was fought on Tuesday Last [August 9] on
the Georgia side of the river between James Lesley, an attorney, and Dr.

Bochelle…Mr Lesley was shot through the body and died in a few hours."
From August 2, 1853: "Duel this morning about 5 o'clock [at] back of the
race course. Mr. J.D. Legare and Mr. Dunovant met to settle their disputes
when the former was instantly killed." And, of course, from May 25, 1839:
"Duel fought at the lower end of Broad Street between Fell and Herriot, the
former shot in the foot to keep him from running and the latter in the mouth
to keep him from jawing."[2]

So why, really, was there so much violence in and around Charleston,
the so-called Holy City? Is the adage true that within the bounds of the
blessed lie the truest of sinners? Some might even suggest it was the heat.
At least that was Charleston's own Dr. David Ramsay's hypothesis in 1809
when he stated that "warm weather and its attendant increase of bile in
the stomach" generated "an irritable temper which made men say and do
things thoughtlessly without any deliberate intention of hurting the feelings
of another person." To be sure, Dr. Ramsay was no dope, far from it in fact.
A 1773 Princeton graduate with a medical degree from the University of
Pennsylvania and a two-time South Carolina delegate to the Continental
Congresses of 1782 and 1785, his contributions to American independence
and its history are exemplary even today.[3]

In truth, Ramsay's thinking does carry some merit, scientific theory or
not. A simple perusal over duels recorded in Charleston during the late
eighteenth and early nineteenth centuries reveals that, indeed, a majority
of them took place between June and September. Noteworthy also is the
public's awareness of these heat-related disputes. An ad placed in the *City
Gazette & Daily Advertiser* by Timothy Crackskull (hopefully a pseudonym)
noted on July 2, 1793:

> *Whereas the warmth that usually prevails in the month of July has very
> strong effects on the constitution of the inhabitants of this city, and as
> amongst many of the young gentlemen it may issue on duels—the subscriber
> gives this public notice, that he has choice and approved pistols, on the
> newest and most destructive construction, which he will hire at the rate of
> one guinea per day for each pair. Enquire at No. 9 Old Church-yard.*

Also in Ramsay's defense, contemporary medical researchers have
initiated numerous studies comparing weather's effects on moods and
actually have found evidence concluding high temperature and humidity
levels as having negative impacts on one's demeanor. One particular
Swedish study in 1974 observed over sixteen thousand college-age students

Dueling Pistols, by Kincheloe, 2012, watercolor. For their contests, South Carolina duelists sometimes chose early morning hours just before sunrise, usually in isolated locations outside of town. A nationally recognized watercolorist and sculptor, Kincheloe's works are included in numerous private and public collections around the country, including the National Museum of Women in the Arts, Washington D.C. *Private collection, photo by Sean Money.*

and recorded notable increases in both dysphoria and irritability. Another analysis performed in 2004 revealed a conclusive bond between aggressive behavior and high humidity—a climactic condition for which Charleston is world renowned.[4]

By modern scientific standards though, blaming *all* local duelists' murderous behavior on the weather seems a bit too easy. Letters, correspondences, court documents and newspaper articles in both the eighteenth and nineteenth centuries specifically comment on the persistent stubbornness among adversaries, their arguments carrying on for months at a time *and* throughout changing seasons. Moreover, plenty of Charleston's duels occurred in non-summer months. Ramsay himself, for instance, was involved with at least one duel in Charleston, serving as an attendant (or second) to Edward Peter Simons in an affair with Gilbert C. Geddes—a duel which occurred in late October 1823.[5]

Besides the weather, dogmatism was a major symptom of a duelist's temperament. After all, for any honorable aristocrat to waver in his beliefs was, for its day, the equivalent of spinelessness. (Politicians even now are harangued loudly for flip-flopping on an issue.) Plenty of stubborn locals gratuitously used newspapers and the perpetual neighborhood rumor mill to assert their rigid convictions—even in the face of hard evidence proving they were mistaken. Seemingly, it was these poor souls who were the most dangerous in Charleston.

In 1807, Thomas Hutson, a local attorney, made a flippantly insulting comment about an associate named Arthur Smith. Smith, upon notification of Hutson's words, took him to task by demanding that he "acknowledge publicly that it is untrue." Of note here is that Hutson and Smith up until this point had been close colleagues, considered by some as longtime friends and courtroom allies. Despite this close relationship, Hutson remained inflexible, exhibiting numb-skulled obstinacy to the point where retraction of any kind was, even among friends, out of the question. He replied to Smith, "I do not recall the remark but if I said it, I meant it."[6]

A challenge followed. The pair met on September 14 at Pigeon Point near Beaufort and exchanged shots. Each fell. Smith died that night, Hutson a few hours later. Both in their early twenties, Hutson's and Smith's funerals were performed concurrently. In perhaps a forewarning to others, both families and attending clergy laid the two to rest in the same tomb.[7]

For likely obvious reasons, dueling in retrospect appears foolish, reckless and even humorous to many. Silly as it may sound today though, it was a deadly serious matter for those who partook of it long ago. Unfortunately, those raw, human emotions that, in turn, led to controlled killing remain impossible to quantify, further clouding our empathy for it now in the twenty-first century. Even more disturbing are the dozens of popular historical figures like Henry Clay and Sam Houston who openly protested the deadly art yet still took part in it. Even Alexander Hamilton went on record as an opponent to dueling, and most everyone knows just how horribly that principle worked out for him.[8]

Sadly, Charlestonians were not used to subservient roles—especially the rich ones. While lower socioeconomic classes answered to the law and more or less respected its enforcement, those of high wealth were a bit more aloof. For them, slander and libel were constant, severe threats, and these character smirches were something that no common courtroom was fit to handle correctly. Or so they believed.

Now, by today's standards, what with social networking, expanded (and relentless) news coverage and a seemingly bottomless chasm of digital information, purposely faulting a person's character is nothing noteworthy. In fact, numbers of reality-based television shows practically wallow in it. Imagine if at the end of each episode of *Survivor* the contestant voted off the island could challenge a teammate, walk off ten paces and shoot him or her. It's simply unheard of. Yet the defamation is still there, the same basic insults and criticisms exist and, worse, it's broadcast all over the country. Of course, human emotions of today run just as high as in past centuries (actually higher judging by the recorded number of antidepressants prescribed in recent years). Yet what is clearly not the same are the consequences of losing face. Honor and character are routinely questioned among countless scores of people on a daily basis, but unlike the upper classes of past centuries, most of modern society has fortunately learned to absorb it and move on.

An overwhelming amount of psychological studies can be launched from observations within dueling's history. Presently, though, it is impossible to ascertain any real *symptoms* of duelists. Did conditions like depression or general anxiety disorders factor in? If so, then to what degree did each influence a duelist's vengefulness? Unfortunately, psychiatric analyses of duelists cannot be performed in hindsight, or at least not accurately. Thus, today's historians likely will never have an exact answer to the essential question: *What were they thinking?*

Finally, Charleston psychiatrist Howard M. Kurtzman, MD, offers a more modern, maybe more understandable retrospection. He observes that the issuing of challenges as well as accepting them was likely done out of nothing more than pure fear—something that Charleston's wealthy elitists had plenty of in those earlier days. He states:

> In essence, a duelist is insecure, and he needs the identification with an unsullied reputation. This false and inflated identity becomes who the duelist actually believes he is. It boosts his value and increases his specialness compared to other men and must be defended at all costs. Attacking this identity is tantamount to being physically assaulted. A fight for one's life/ identity is the only remedy to the perceived loss in his value. Winning such a high-stakes duel would not only restore the loss but, depending on the publicity generated, also boost his value even higher than it was before the insult. In my opinion, the winner of a duel has, in essence, shot himself, and his "victory," if any, is indeed Pyrrhic.[9]

Just as Kurtzman says, within the conventions of a gentleman, honor was valued higher than life itself. Lose honor, lose everything. It was a frightful

Duel au pistolet au XIXème siècle, by Bauce et Rouget in 1857 denotes a traditional *affaire d'honneur* among gentlemen. Each duelist is using a flintlock pistol, is clothed in proper attire and has an assistant on hand to govern the fight. A surgeon is ready to administer care to the loser. *Courtesy of Wikimedia Commons/public domain.*

notion indeed. As Shakespeare wrote, "Life every man holds dear, but the dear man holds Honor far more precious-dear than life."[10]

Fear of ridicule, then, or a tarnished repute in the eyes of one's peers led to bitter resentment and an overbearing *need* to right the wrong. This resentment, Kurtzman continues, subsequently brooded within, eventually boiling over into vengeance. Vengeance then systematically took over rationalization to the point where any inner reflection on the consequences (i.e., dying) was the furthest thing from a duelist's mind. Attain satisfaction first and damn whatever else happens. Whatever the motives, Charleston citizens and soldiers alike were excellent students of revenge and justice. Their personal integrity and conviction proved paramount, and they killed— sometimes brutally—to preserve both.

Without question, it's extraordinarily tough to pinpoint Charleston's (maybe even South Carolina's) most well-known duel. For starters, one must at least consider the feud and ultimate 1778 showdown between Charleston's Christopher Gadsden and Major General Robert Howe. So well known was that particular affair that a song was written about it. A few verses, sung to the tune of "Yankee Doodle":

> *And then they both together made,*
> *This honest declaration—*
> *That they came here by honor led,*
> *And not by inclination.*
>
> *That is, they fought, 'twas not because*
> *Of rancor, spite or passion,*
> *But only to obey the laws*
> *Of custom and the fashion.*
>
> *The pistols then, before their eyes,*
> *Were fairly primed and loaded;*
> *H. wished and so did G. likewise,*
> *The custom was exploded.*[11]

Maybe best remembered today as a founder of Charleston's Sons of Liberty and designer of the Gadsden flag (Don't Tread On Me), Christopher Gadsden was a Charleston-born merchant and militia captain before the outset of the American Revolutionary War. After completing studies in England, Gadsden returned to America and began a professional career in Philadelphia. His impressive business achievements there provided him the necessary means to return to his Charleston home in 1747.

While his mercantile achievements were noteworthy, they paled in comparison to his political and military careers. Gadsden played a major role in South Carolina's blossoming state government. In 1778, he acted as vice-president of South Carolina (now known as lieutenant governor) and was a vital constituent in the convention to draft a new state constitution. It was in this same year, regrettably, that Gadsden found himself on the dueling grounds facing a fellow military officer, Robert Howe.

A major general in the Continental army with ancestral ties to Charleston, Howe was no stranger to social or political strife. Once called "a horrid animal" by a female acquaintance, he was terrible with money and even worse with women. What's more, although a diligent and qualified officer, circumstances beyond his control during the American Revolution caused

A portrait of Christopher Gadsden by Jeremiah Theus, circa 1765. *Courtesy of the Charleston Museum.*

him extraordinary hardship on the battlefield. More than once his own troops turned on him. By mid-1778, with the British's southern campaign in high gear, there arose once more a palpable fear of redcoats and Hessians marching into Charleston. Many were still brooding over Howe's abandonment of Savannah and were none too pleased to now have him in town commanding the Southern Department.

Understandably concerned for the future, Gadsden quickly brought Howe's military leadership and soldierly skills into question. In a searing letter dated July 4, 1778, Gadsden berated Howe on various points, including his ability to follow orders, his overall military authority and his credibility as a man. Letting his temper take control, Gadsden circulated the letter publicly, and it was not long before Howe issued a challenge citing a public besmirching of his character.

With Gadsden refusing to retract his statements, the two ultimately met in a pasture near the west end of present-day Spring Street on the morning of August 30, 1778. Ignoring customary rules of silence while in position, Gadsden goaded Howe that he "ought to begin the entertainment."[12]

Howe eagerly obliged. Taking aim, he sent a .50-caliber lead slug hurtling downfield, barely missing Gadsden's face. As the bang echoed and faded, Gadsden remained motionless and silent. Unhurt, the sobering realization of his wrongdoing (and how close he had just come to his own grave) sank in. After a brief moment of self-contemplation, Gadsden purposely discharged his pistol harmlessly away from Howe. This action of course should have ended the matter once and for all, but in an amazing show of either extreme humility or just stupid bravado, Gadsden called on Howe to reload and shoot at him again. Thankfully, Howe had had enough and proclaimed his satisfaction. The two shook hands and left.

As for the rest of South Carolina, it is hard to ignore the Cash-Shannon contest near Bishopville. This contest, recognized as the last fatal duel in South Carolina, occurred over a century after the Gadsden-Howe ordeal on July 5, 1880, and with spectators numbering in the hundreds (plenty of them journalists), it is probably the most well-documented duel in the state.

Admittedly, the causes of this particular spat are a bit convoluted, involving assorted lawsuits, ensuing settlements and a cast of individuals all run amok. In any case, the blame game between Colonels Ellerbe B.C. Cash of Chesterfield and William M. Shannon of Camden dragged on for twenty-seven months, spiraling more and more violently out of control. Further adding to the vitriol were allegations of monetary shenanigans and fraud against Cash's wife, causing her such embarrassment and shame that on April 19, 1880, she "was stricken speechless and died."[13]

Now, whatever the scientific cause of Mrs. Cash's death, it was long lauded that bringing family members (especially females) into any argument was a serious step over the bounds of decency. Cash was furious and out for blood.

His challenge to duel was accepted by Colonel Shannon, and the two eventually met by Lynches River. Well dressed and exhibiting all the proper mannerisms that had been decided upon, the adversaries exchanged pleasantries, took their arranged places on the field, leveled their pistols at each other and fired. Within minutes, Shannon, a father of fourteen children, was dead.

News of the duel permeated papers up and down the East Coast, including the *New York Times*, which noted, "The affair was conducted according to the code of honor, and regular dueling pistols were used…There is no doubt that the murder of Shannon was determined on from the outset." If nothing else, Shannon's death finally brought to bear the realities of dueling and its supposed senselessness in the post–Civil War South, a new country still reeling from Reconstruction and no longer tolerant of private, prideful violence.

Unfortunately, as endemic as dueling might have been among Charleston's private citizens, fighting amid its military ranks was equally troubling. Lord William Campbell, first royal governor of the colony, proclaimed to Lord Dartmouth in 1775, "Charles Town is the fountainhead from which all violence flows." Though he was speaking of rebellious-minded Charlestonians, his comment could have been easily justified were it directed at the infighting of its military defenders. Like the clash between Gadsden and Howe, dueling among soldiers was a considerable problem in times of both peace and war.[14]

William Moultrie, Nathanael Greene and even George Washington all opposed the custom for the obvious fact that soldiers wounded or killed while dueling was detrimental to military's ultimate strengths, and these three were in constant need of as many able-bodied soldiers as they could get. Still, officers boldly (albeit irresponsibly) often took to the dueling fields against one of their own. On June 19, 1818, for example, the *Charleston Courier* noted:

> *We understand that a duel took place, at Castle Pinckney in this harbour, on Wednesday evening last, between Lieut. Caldwell, first of the U.S. Schr.* Lynx, *and Lieut. Taylor, second of the brig* Prometheus, *in which the former received a flesh wound in the body. It is to be lamented that gentlemen who have, on all occasions, displayed the utmost bravery when engaged with the enemies of their country, should conceive it necessary so frequently in vindication of their character to resort to this murderous expedient—this being the third or fourth instance within the last six months, on the Southern station. Nothing, probably, short of cashiering both the principals engaged in a Duel will put an end to the barbarous custom.*

Unsurprisingly, most chivalric military leaders embraced the principles of dueling instead of decrying it, and those trained under the auspices of British imperialism fit the mold nicely. Needing to defend one of its most valuable colonies amid the Anglo-Cherokee War, Parliament in 1761 assigned a corps of British regulars under the command of Colonel James Grant to South Carolina to assist Colonel Thomas Middleton's standing provincial regiment. Feeling shirked of his military influence, Middleton publicly (and repeatedly) condemned Grant for overreaching the bounds of his authority and for exhibiting "a most offensive indifference to all the suggestions of the provincial officers."[15]

Beginning in March, an expedition against the Cherokee led by Grant and Middleton was underway. Throughout the campaign, hostility between Grant's regulars and Middleton's provincials brewed deeply. Further adding to Middleton's hatred, Grant proceeded to crush the natives mercilessly, wiping out herds of livestock, destroying crops and burning entire Cherokee villages to the ground. Upon their return, Middleton was even more infuriated with Grant, who, in his arrogance, took full credit for the success of the mission.[16]

Finally, by December, Middleton was fed up. In an act of uncontrollable rage, he attacked Grant with a cane on Charleston's Vendue Range. Grant knew his only recourse to such a bodily assault was to duel. Although not much is known about the actual gunfight, both Grant and Middleton survived the contest. Interestingly though, Grant later stated in a letter, "I gave him his Life, when it was Absolutely in my Power." This line suggests that Grant may have intentionally missed.[17]

Military dueling only escalated during the time of the American Revolution. General William Moultrie's memoirs, for example, include a letter to Captain George Turner, in which he discusses scores of Patriot soldiers imprisoned at Haddrell's Point not long after Charleston's surrender to the British in 1780. Moultrie writes:

> *The officers, prisoners at Haddrell's-point were very ungovernable indeed, and it was not much to be wondered at, when two hundred and fifty of them from different states, were huddled up together in the barracks, many of them of different dispositions, and some of them very uncouth gentlemen; it is not surprising that there should be continual disputes among them, and frequent duels.*[18]

Likewise, in a letter from Nathanael Greene to Governor Alexander Martin dated November 25, 1781, the general made his concerns for dueling within the ranks particularly clear. Greene writes of the Marquis de Malmedy, a French officer killed in a duel while serving with the southern army: "The fate of Col Malmedy I supposed you will have heard before this can reach you. He lost his life by that stupid custom which has in many instances disgraced the history of the American war and deprived the public of the services of several valuable men."[19]

Sad as it was, the gentleman's duel remained a sophisticated ritual cherished among the armed forces prior to and during the Civil War. Midshipmen Archibald H. Waring of Charleston and James J. Waddell, a North Carolinian, were doubtlessly aware of the duelist code of conduct. In fact, the United States Navy included a full transcript of the Irish-written *Code Duello* (a tutorial of sorts printed in 1777 listing rules and recommendations on proper dueling) in its midshipman's handbook in 1778, and it stayed there until the navy finally banned dueling among its ranks in 1862. On May 27, 1842, while in Norfolk, Virginia, aboard the USS *Pennsylvania*, the two agreed to settle their score "caused by a young lady." Thanks to a misfire, Waring was unhurt. Waddell, however, was shot in the hip and carried a limp the rest of his life.[20]

Throughout the years, many contests, depending on the argument, ended peacefully. Others most certainly did not. But whatever the historic outcomes, Charleston still carries an undeniably abundant history of duelists and dueling that began almost immediately at the time of its founding.

Chapter 2
Judicium Dei

In the Beginning

Duellum, an antiquated form of *bellum* meaning war or combat, appears in literature not long after the fall of the Roman Empire. Medieval Latin correspondences regard it as singular combat under the management of a governing body, although the definition of dueling in any English-language dictionary has remained essentially unchanged for centuries: "A prearranged combat between two persons fought with deadly weapons according to an accepted code of procedure" set aside for matters within private conflicts.[21]

It is no secret. Humans—like most all other organisms on earth—are a combative bunch. However examined, a duel is little more than a fight—but at least it is a *really* good-looking one.

Certainly, dueling is nothing new within the realm of world history, and to be sure, it has likely existed in one form or another since early man began throwing rocks at one another. Furthermore, cultural history has always embraced, if not glorified, great rivals: David-Goliath, Achilles-Hector, Teach-Maynard, Ali-Frazier, Vader-Kenobi—duelists all! Shakespeare himself wrote of duels both in his own time and among the ancients. From *Antony and Cleopatra*:

> *He calls me boy; and chides, as he had power*
> *To beat me out of Egypt; my messenger*
> *He hath whipp'd with rods; dares me to personal combat,*
> *Caesar to Antony: let the old ruffian know*

I have many other ways to die; meantime
Laugh at his challenge.[22]

It was not until the more recent eighteenth and nineteenth centuries that dueling truly came into its own as an art, a near perfectly choreographed dance, as it were, aimed (literally) at the disposal of a social enemy. Even in the earliest days of the Charles Towne colony, public perception of dueling was that it was a necessary evil. Even the attitudes of the eight founding Lords Proprietors, though possessing lawful influence over the colony, remained a tad nonchalant toward dueling, not to mention just about any other form of killing. This in spite of tough so-called English Statutes of Force passed circa 1712 that declared any duelist who succeeded in killing his opponent as automatically guilty of (at least) manslaughter and subsequently punished.[23]

Despite rules though, the proprietors appeared far more comfortable raking in cash from the colony's raw materials and not so much nurturing their new region into a well-intentioned utopia. As a result, whatever authority they might have hoped to administer was impossible to enforce and consequently ignored outright among the colonists. From a settler's point of view, how should (or could) laws be imposed from a governing body some four thousand miles beyond the horizon? Thus, dueling in Charleston began early and occurred often.

Likely, the first duel fought on South Carolina soil was one between John Stewart and Captain Job Howe. Although little is known of Captain Howe (an ancestor of the aforementioned Robert Howe), he was listed in a 1683 census report, making him among the first pioneering settlers to the Charles Towne peninsular region. Mr. Stewart appears to have been the overseer of Wadboo Barony near the Biggin and Wadboo Creeks close to present-day Lake Moultrie and was furthermore recorded as an "Indian trader and expansionist."[24]

In the spring of 1690, Howe publicly and repeatedly slandered Stewart as an "ill adviser" to the provincial governor, James Colleton. Not long after, in keeping to their English heritage, the two agreed to meet with swords. In a letter to Major William Dunlop dated April 27, 1690, Stewart writes, "I prepar'd myselfe and next mor'g [when we met] drew on him…We went to the woods [and] drew in a glen…We were standing 6 minutes with sword to sword 2 foot within 'other." As the fight began, however, witnesses to the duel intervened and restrained both Howe and Stewart. Then, as Stewart continues, "Being stop'd by two constables…[Howe] cam up basely and struck me with a hickory stick upon which I…drew my scymeter [meaning scimitar, a curved-blade backsword] and run after How and mist my stroak within an Inch of his neck, so he became the mockery of the town." In closing, Stewart made it clear, "They like not my Scymeter and I shall far sooner sacrefice a life subject to so many Misfortunes rather then enjoy life with dishonor."[25]

Naturally, to understand best the nature of a more modern duel, or at least those recognizable *affaires d'honneur* most romanticized in present-day vernacular, one must look well past the last few centuries of Charleston or even American histories. Obviously, dueling among well-heeled southern gentlemen did not just sprout up alongside New World discoveries and American colonialism. In fact, for Charleston and the rest of the country, fighting based on principle and character was a familiar event, and these so-called duels of honor can credit their origins to the very popular, very bloody and very legal contests of antiquity.

In this broad epoch—one certainly known for its bloody events—a duel among adversaries was an involved and detailed arrangement requiring law, order and above all, of course, the Almighty. Those defamed, accused or wronged in some way could by right request a defense of their integrity by means of hand-to-hand battle. This early version of dueling was practiced initially among Germanic tribes throughout Continental Europe as "judicial combat" or sometimes "trial by combat," "ordeal by combat" or "ritual combat." While evidence of these contests first appeared in ancient Burgundian laws circa AD 501, they eventually made their way into all European monarchies, eventually spreading to England via the Anglo-Saxon and Norman invasions, where they were more widely adapted as "wagers of battle."[26]

The basis of these contests was, at its core, fairly simple: when no clear evidence or witnesses to a crime or dispute could be produced, a contest or a combative examination of sorts was carried out publicly amongst spectators, clergy and respective governing officials. After petitioning their case to a ruler, two opposing arguers could be granted a one-on-one battle tribunal. The use of weapons, be they daggers, long swords, heavy axes, spears or plain bare hands, was agreed upon before the opponents finally set upon each other to literally fight it out amongst themselves.

Now, at a time of supreme ecclesiastical authority, it was universally understood that God's will alone chose both the victor and the vanquished. Be it in a war or just a mundane argument, it was collectively *believed* that the right or correct man would emerge victorious not by his own cunning or skill as a fighter but rather from *Judicium Dei* or judgment from

God. In effect, judicial combat was a direct appeal to God. He himself would judge absolutely, unconditionally and correctly. As a result, only the righteous could win. Unfortunately, also made clear by this divine decision was, of course, the loser. An accused man defeated in judicial combat was judged instantly guilty of whatever crime he was charged and thereafter punished accordingly.

Conversely, should the plaintiff (or demandant, as he was called) find himself bested, he was promptly deemed "liable to the penalties that would have fallen upon the accused." For instance, one of the earliest wagers of battle to transpire in England recorded the Count of Eu, pitted against one Godefroi Baynard. Upon accusing Baynard of conspiracy to murder, Count d'Eu was (eventually) granted a venue with which to challenge Baynard but was soundly defeated in the fight that followed. Thus, in the eyes of the law and the church, Baynard was innocent and proclaimed so by the king. As for the count, for his trouble he was "cruelly mutilated" under royal command.[27]

Expectedly, historic descriptions of these affairs tend to reek of the ultra-violent gladiatorial clashes of classical Rome, but even though the fights were similar, governance of them differed. For example, common rules throughout certain regions of Europe exempted individuals commonly found unqualified for fighting. Among these were men aged fewer than twenty or over sixty years, women, ranking clerics, the sick, the wounded or disfigured or the otherwise just infirm.[28]

However, it was certainly permissible (encouraged even) for one of these persons to hire out should they find themselves in a dispute. Contracted champions, fighters-for-a-fee so to speak, were available to do battle on behalf of the unfit contestant, but unlike the tournament-style, arena death shows for which the Romans cheered, judicial combats were a serious matter that, in effect, piously judged a person's guilt or innocence. Unsurprisingly, different cultures all through Europe possessed varying interpretations of this government-controlled fighting. In some areas, hand-to-hand carnage settled just as many minor civil suits as criminal cases.[29]

In England, a contestant could defeat his opponent in one of two ways under the trial rules of the eleventh and twelfth centuries. Of course, the ideal strategy was just to kill him, but failing that, the combatant could force his adversary into voluntary submission. Either way, achieving victory was often a brutal and grisly process. Under royal decree, no tactics were off limits; eye gouging, scratching, hair pulling and especially biting were all fair strategies. In fact, English jurist Henry de Bracton noted in the thirteenth century that front incisors provided quite an advantage since "teeth of that kind help greatly to victory," and one particular combat in 1456 notes that two fighters "with their teeth...tore [each other's flesh] like dragons."[30]

During this same time, a noteworthy byproduct of the English wager battles emerged. Sometime after the tenth century (once knighthoods had developed in earnest), so-called duels of chivalry became not only terrific problem solvers for knights in dispute but also eventual honored ceremonies among nobles. As it was, knights with all their rank and power had a great deal to lose in terms of honor. Under the mega-oppressive statutes of feudalism, especially within the Anglo-Norman culture, social order was an omnipresent, all-important way of life.

With war and bloodshed at their nuclei, armored knights most assuredly enjoyed their place in the upper echelons of society. Bred in the ways of chivalric law, these were men adept in the ways of warfare and skilled in all manner of edged weapons. In fact, it was mostly through battle that knights rose through the ranks of the landed gentry. Simply put, the more blood a knight spilled, the greater his eminence and social dominance. Alexis de Tocqueville reflected on the violence of feudal knighthood, writing in the 1830s:

> In some cases, feudal honor enjoined revenge, and stigmatized forgiveness of insults; in others it imperiously commanded men to conquer their own passions, and imposed forgetfulness of self. It did not make humanity or kindness its law...it preferred great crimes to small earnings; cupidity was less distasteful to it than avarice; violence it often sanctioned, but cunning and treachery it invariably reprobated as contemptible.[31]

To be sure, gore-spattered armor and blood-drenched blades were not detriments as much as they were symbols of valiance to the knights. Richard the Lionheart, for instance, had a particularly nasty habit of splitting opponents' skulls "down to the teeth" and was all the more revered for it. Today, no one really studies Robert the Bruce's political prowess in Scotland, but military historians still retell his masterful axe-wielding wallop that destroyed Henry de Bohun's head at the Battle of Bannockburn in 1314.[32]

Amidst all this bloodlust then, it comes as no surprise that knights eagerly took to dueling, especially in times of peace. After all, if armed conflict was at the center of a knight's socioeconomic universe, how else was he to stay relevant at times when there were no wars to fight? Since theirs was a time when slaughter brought about significance, barons and ranking gentlemen

An Italian woodcut, circa 1400, by Christine de Pisan depicting hand-to-hand combat among armored knights and nobles. *Courtesy of Library of Congress.*

in conflict with each other often engaged in savage clashes, taking up arms against each other at will and immune to any feudal justice systems.

So popular were these duels of chivalry, in fact, that nobles and members of royalty set up tournaments to highlight an individual's combative skills and prowess. Tournaments of arms were incredibly grand affairs and could carry on for weeks at a time. The events summoned crowds throughout the country, and rulers frequently ordered them usually in some observance of a national event, perhaps a royal birthday or anniversary.

Early tournaments were for the most part safe, employing altered weapons and protective rules. Unfortunately, spectators soon tired of the tameness, and bona fide battle instruments entered into play. One can easily guess the repercussions of such a change, but at least it gave the audience something exciting to watch. In 1468, for instance, Edward IV held a tournament celebrating the marriage of his sister to the Duke of Burgundy. For the finale, a group of twenty well-armed knights and nobles faced off against an opposing group of equal number. The match quickly turned into a bloody free-for-all, at last forcing King Edward to call in troops to separate them. Of course, there was also the unfortunate 1559 jousting mishap of King

Le Tournoy où le Royl fenryn fut blefse a mort le dernier de luin.1559.

A sixteenth-century woodcut illustrating Henri II of France receiving a mortal head wound during a 1559 celebration tournament that he himself ordered. In a jousting match with Gabriel Montgomery, a large, jagged fragment from Montgomery's shattered lance passed through Henri's helmet visor and lodged in his skull. Henri II died twelve days later. *Private collection, photo by Sean Money.*

Henri II, who was killed during his own tournament by a member of the Scottish Guards.[33]

In a period known for violence, sanctioned judicial combats, wagers of battle and duels of chivalry at least did a decent job of preventing men (and sometimes women) from killing in the throes of passion. Weeks or sometimes months would pass before judges allowed a contest to commence, giving the adversaries ample time to work things out on their own. Henry I of England declared that the practice of judicial combat was "enacted with consent and applause of many faithful bishops" and, in his opinion, was the nearest thing to an infallible court system England had ever known.[34]

Despite its cruelty and admittedly dubious conclusions, it remained a standard form of prevailing justice well into the Elizabethan period. Dreadfully, it was not until an act of Parliament in 1819 that wagers of battle were formally outlawed. Eighteenth-century Scottish historian William Robertson wrote in retrospect:

By this barbarous custom, the natural course of proceeding, both in civil and criminal questions, was entirely perverted. Force usurped the place of equity in courts of judicature, and justice was banished from her proper mansion. Discernment, learning, integrity, were qualities less necessary to a judge than bodily strength and dexterity in the use of arms.[35]

By the 1600s, mortal combats had begun a gradual evolution away from government arenas and into somewhat more private affairs complete with protocol and appointed intermediaries. Within a short period, areas of Western Europe, primarily England, Spain and France, had neatly transformed the duel into more of a ritualistic concern and not so much an all-out brawl. Even as late as 1865, Mark Twain wrote about such contrasts while traveling:

This pastime is as common in Austria today as it is in France. But with this difference—that here in the Austrian states the duel is dangerous, while in France it is not. Here it is tragedy, in France it is comedy; here it is a solemnity, there it is monkeyshines; here the duelist risks his life, there he does not even risk his shirt. Here he fights with pistol or saber, in France with a hairpin—a blunt one. Here the desperately wounded man tries to walk to the hospital; there they paint the scratch so that they can find it again, lay the sufferer on a stretcher, and conduct him off the field with a band of music.[36]

Twain's remarks, while perhaps apropos for the 1860s, are a tad inaccurate when applied to French gentlemen of earlier eras. For example, during the reign of Henry IV of France (1589–1610), it is estimated that between four and six thousand dueling fatalities occurred within one decade. There, a sharp sword was ostensibly more *en vogue* than any furnishing or garment, and for more than one hundred years it served as "the universal arbiter." Fortunately, as French fashion changed so did its enthusiasm for fighting. Despite this fade, however, the country never completely abandoned its dueling bravado (a repute that would reemerge dramatically in its American colony of New Orleans).[37]

Conversely, in other parts of Europe, countries like Italy and Malta for example, deaths among duelists were rare. While Italian duelists certainly adhered to the chivalric laws of their ancestors and were indeed among the finest swordsmen anywhere, duels there were typically satisfied after first blood was drawn. Safer still, the Maltese had a unique written law declaring that any duel was to cease upon "the request or command of a woman, ecclesiastic, or a knight."[38]

Naturally, as with most English or European exports, dueling had no trouble immigrating to the American colonies. In fact, it arrived on practically the first boat to drop anchor in Massachusetts. Famously, the first duel fought within the confines of the New World happened here in 1621—barely one year after the arrival at Plymouth. The duel, carried out with swords, pitted Edward Leicester and Edward Doty against each other before a band of witnesses and various attendants. In the end, each man was injured and bloodied but managed to walk away without assistance.

Interestingly, the Leicester-Doty affair represents (perhaps unfortunately) just one of many changes dueling would undergo in its transition from Europe to the American colonies—this despite its deathless finale. From the Middle Ages up until this particular fight, dueling was performed solely within society's upper crust. Strangely enough, however, Leicester and Doty were indentured servants, making their participation in a formal duel a blatant disregard for all classical convention. Therefore, in one swipe of a sword, this one duel effortlessly set a new, albeit substandard, precedent for dueling in America.

For the most part, duels of the American colonial, federal and Victorian periods remained anchored in high standards among those within a certain socioeconomic rank. Even though the armored knights of old had physically evolved into landed elites by the turn of the seventeenth century, their mental ideals of honor and chivalry remained the same. Most among Charleston's upper classes nourished the tradition of dueling, in fact making it an integral part of their social guidance. It was an important matter of taste and caste. For generations gentlemen revered it as an almost holy rite. Even as late as 1889—nine years after dueling fell into extinction in South Carolina—locals continued to honor their ancestors' combative yet honorable days of yore. Colonel John Cunningham wrote in Charleston's *Daily Sun* newspaper on October 1:

> *We refer to that trial of the Middle Ages…according to which it was the custom for the accused and the accuser to do battle in proof of the right, the defeat of the one or the other to sustain or disprove the justice of the accusation. Of course, the event of such a trial was directed more by the comparative skill, strength, and nerve of the respective combatants than by the merits of the cause, notwithstanding that God was popularly believed to give the victory to the righteous side, and element which does not enter into the calculations of the duelist.*

Chapter 3

Prelude to a Duel

Wars of Words and Whereabouts

Before his duel with John Edwards, Dennis O'Driscoll sat down and wrote out his will:

> *Charleston Augt 9ᵗʰ 1817. This my Will—*
> *I do pray God of his infinite mercy and goodness to pardon all my sins: and forgive me for the Conduct I am about to pursue, to which I have been forced after every possible endeavor on my part to avoid it; and* [should it] *please Almighty God that I shd.' fall a victim to defence of my character & my Honor; I will & devise all my estate or property of which I am now possessed, or may be entitled to, to my most dear & affectionate Wife Harriett C. O'Driscoll, & I pray God to grant her firmness to withstand her misfortune.*[39]

The two fought eight days later. O'Driscoll was shot and killed.

So what constitutes a duel *really*? That is, what makes up the time-honored mystique of two men so enthralled in their convictions that they physically make an earnest attempt to kill each other? Character and virtue were, needless to say, of utmost importance to Charlestonians in the eighteenth and nineteenth centuries. The city itself was a veritable nucleus of culture and wealth all based on strong family lineages, heralded ties to mother England and a thriving plantation-based economy.

The urban center of Charleston was furthermore a bustling hub of activity. Besides huge maritime commerce, Charleston was a virtual asylum for artisans beginning not long after the settlement moved to its permanent location on the peninsula in 1680. In 1762, *London Magazine* called the city "one of the richest in America," and Josiah Quincy himself wrote of Charleston that same year: "This town makes a most beautiful appearance as you come up to it, and in many respects a magnificent one...in grandeur, splendor of buildings, decorations, equipages, numbers, commerce, shipping, indeed in almost everything, it far surpasses all I ever saw or expected to see in America."[40]

In fact, just before the eventual surrender (and subsequent occupation) of the city by British military forces in 1780, there were twenty-five silversmiths, goldsmiths and jewelers working in Charleston. By 1820, the number had increased to nearly eighty. From 1740 to 1750, the number of cabinetmakers in the city had doubled—and doubled again by 1760. By 1800, sixty-three cabinetmakers were making their living here. By 1810, there were eighty-one listed in the directories. This is a staggering number. Put against the urban geography of Charleston from 1810 to 1840, there could have easily existed one to as many as three cabinetmaking, metal-smithing and jeweler shops per acre. These numbers certainly attest to the strength of Charleston's economy and commercial market of the eighteenth and nineteenth centuries based on not just an agricultural empire but also a large export trade and a steady, loyal patronage of local clientele.[41]

It is unsurprising then that because of this overwhelming wealth and civility within Charleston, one's reputation was of serious concern. Duels in the Carolina Lowcountry were, at least in most circumstances, fought over the usual: insults to one's moral makeup or slurs toward one's honor, character or family lineage. These usually served well as grounds for a challenge, and the receiver of such ridicule was all but expected to retaliate. One South Carolina newspaper editorial appearing in the *Anderson Intelligencer* put it succinctly in November 1894: "The man who was challenged to fight a duel and even wavered one second in accepting it was forever socially damned, branded, ostracized forever and ever."

Indeed, many Charlestonians of the day considered slander a physical attack on one's person just as European-born traditions had long dictated. In his observations of honor among Americans, for example, Alexis de Tocqueville wrote in 1840:

> *It would seem that men employ two very distinct methods in the public estimations of their fellowmen; at one time they judge them by those simple notions of right and wrong which are diffused all over the world; at*

another they refer their decision to a few very special notions which belong exclusively to some particular age and country...Honor, at the periods of its greatest power, sways the will more than the belief of men and even whilst they yield without hesitation and without a murmur to it dictates, they feel notwithstanding, by a dim but mighty instinct, the existence of a more general, more ancient, and more holy law, which they sometimes disobey although they cease not to acknowledge it.[42]

At a time when so much as one unfavorable rumor could result in serious social injury or economic damage, it henceforth became the job of each individual to protect himself from slander. Thus, many in Charleston and elsewhere around the state viewed dueling as a mechanism of self-defense. Even though there were assorted laws during the colonial period offering protection from defamation, the thought of pressing charges of such was petty among the elites. Running off to the authorities over hurt feelings revealed one's own thin skin and fragile mindset, a character flaw of a gutless fool. A man, they believed, was responsible for his own person. He should defend it violently—and by whatever means necessary.

As for those gentrified Charlestonians who had been verbally wronged, it was after one of them *believed* himself insulted that slander and libel laws became irrelevant and the real, ceremonial modus operandi of dueling commenced. Offended parties made no secret of their feelings, and often enough, ancillary allies and enemies got into the fray. In Charleston, beliefs and traditions were deeply anchored in the rites of medieval Europe in that only those of upper-class wealth and status were suitable for carrying out their affairs on a field of honor. Customarily then, before any challenge ensued, great care was taken by both parties to ensure their opponent was at least of equal status and, therefore, a viable candidate for a duel. Perhaps the most famous occurrence of this strict adherence to equality was the notorious 1856 beating of Massachusetts senator Charles Sumner by South Carolina's own Preston Smith Brooks.

On May 20, 1854, Charles Sumner made a blistering speech on the House floor railing against the Kansas-Nebraska Act and relentlessly slandering its fabricators, Stephen A. Douglas and Andrew Butler. Completely offended by the lecture, Brooks quietly voiced his desire to challenge Sumner to a duel over the remarks. However, Laurence Keitt, a fellow South Carolina congressman and Fire-Eater from Orangeburg, made note to Brooks that Sumner might not be a worthy opponent. Keitt further reminded Brooks of a specific section in the *Royal Code of Honor* that stated, "If my adversary be a worthless man, I shall degrade my own character effectually by placing it upon a level with his." Keitt also consented to Brooks that, based on the grotesque sexual innuendos made by Sumner in his speech, the Yankee senator was of far lower social status, comparable to that of a worthless drunk. A mere plebeian, as it were.[43] It was all Brooks needed to hear.

Brooks knew that within the ritualistic confines of proper dueling etiquette, he could not in good moral character issue a challenge with anyone considered to be a lesser man than himself. By issuing a challenge then, Brooks risked either elevating Sumner's social status or, worse, lowering his own. Furthermore, in the entirety of Sumner's rants, in which he proceeded to lambaste just about every southerner within earshot, at no time did he verbally attack Brooks *personally*. By virtue of dueling, then, it would have been an unacceptable contest.

Unfortunately (for Sumner anyway), Brooks decided the only proper thing to do was to approach the old man from Massachusetts and, with cane in hand, beat him mercilessly with it.

Now, on the surface it appeared to most southerners that Brooks was merely honoring the duelist's decorum. In reality though, Brooks was no dummy when it came to duels and certainly knew the dangers of getting involved in one. Actually, Brooks himself had been wounded several years prior in 1840 during his own duel with Louis T. Wigfall, a native of Edgefield, South Carolina, and eventual Texas senator. Shot in the leg, it was the whole reason Brooks carried a cane in the first place! Certainly it can be believed that Brooks's limp served him well as a reminder to avoid duels when at all possible, perhaps even giving him the excuse he needed to flog Sumner to within an inch of his life.

In this same argument of equality, men often took additional measures of ensuring both a man's social status and ultimate resolve. Adversaries many times took to posting as a means of inviting a duel. Posting, as it was known among duelists primarily in the nineteenth century, served as a psychological strike, a vicious tactic most feared by those wishing to avoid a potentially fatal duel. By posting, one person could publicly voice his displeasure over another in print—usually in the newspaper or by simply placing placards on poles around town.

Naturally, once a person posted a grievance against another, the whole argument was out in the open. Thus, preservation of honor and character became all the more vital. To carry an argument into the community was a mean show of will. For the poor soul on the receiving end of a post, to back down or apologize once the whole affair went public (and in print no

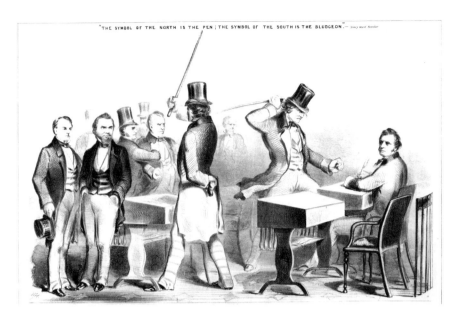

On May 22, 1856, Preston Brooks caned Charles Sumner, who was seated at his desk. Laurence Keitt is shown standing guard to Brooks's right. A quotation from Henry Ward Beecher is printed across the top: "The symbol of the north is the pen; the symbol of the south is the bludgeon." *Courtesy of Library of Congress.*

less) signaled nothing less than moral weakness or, worse, cowardice. Local newspapers, furthermore, only added fuel to the fires. Editors almost always entered the row once a post was placed, printing both accusations and rebuttals from involved parties. Sure enough, once a war of words began, there was practically no stopping it.

Historically, public postings accomplished little. If anything, in fact, they tended to make matters exponentially worse. The posts traded between Charleston attorney Edward Peter Simons and Gilbert C. Geddes, for example, did an excellent job of aggrandizing their initial dispute. On October 4, 1823, an enraged Simons used the *Charleston Mercury and Morning Advertiser* as a tool to rebuke several handbills previously posted about town by Geddes claiming that Simons had insulted his father. Simons printed that he had no recollection of the conversation, writing, "I did not hold myself responsible to the young man for any expressions I may have used in relation to his father…I expressed distinctly that if I had trespassed on the feelings or reflected on the character of [Geddes's father] I held myself responsible to him, and not to any of his family or friends. I repeat this declaration to the public."

Unfortunately, Simons's editorial was no good in the eyes of Geddes, and the postings continued from both sides. Frustrated and fed up with Simons's coyness, Geddes stuck letter-sized placards on various lampposts and walls "in all corners of the city," calling Simons a "Poltroon" and "a coward." With that, the die was cast, and Simons finally published a challenge to Geddes by way of the *Charleston Mercury*.[44]

In the end, numerous postings and editorials exchanged between the two rivals served well in ballooning a once simple misunderstanding of who-said-what into a veritable death match. It was clear that no settlement short of bloodshed would suffice for the two, and someone was going to have to take a bullet before the matter could rest. A letter written by a supposed witness to the duel named Stephen West Moore on October 15, 1823, described the ferocity of the fight between Geddes and Simons:

> *The Parties went down to Fort Johnson on Monday morning the 6th…* *They fought at 12 o'clock and fired four times each, without wounding one another, although the balls cut their clothing. On the fifth round, Geddes was shot through both thighs and Simons in the belly just over the hip. The anxiety for the event was extreme and general in town, and when it was known that both were wounded dangerously, many silly reports were put in circulation.*[45]

Geddes survived the duel but just barely. Simons, on the other hand, died from his wound.

Volatile political and editorial disagreements abounded within Charleston during the Revolutionary eighteenth and secessionist nineteenth centuries. Rival candidates, party members and newspapermen routinely posted each other and passed written challenges demanding satisfaction. The papers were fervent in publicly announcing the grievances of each. As for Charleston's politicos and newspaper editors in the age of dueling, theirs was a particularly dangerous life. Each was especially vulnerable in that these men were already well-known public (and opinionated) figures, and it was not altogether unusual for printed narratives to morph from responsible pieces of journalism into blunt-force invectives. Thus, editors dueled their rival editors over the basis of their respective editorial opinions—a fight begetting a fight.

Benjamin Franklin Timothy (named for his grandfather's friend and mentor) was the son of Lewis Timothy, editor of the *South Carolina Gazette* and third-generation editor in Charleston. Collaborating with William

Mason, the pair created a more modern version of his father's newspaper and on January 1, 1794, released the first edition of the *South Carolina State Gazette and Timothy and Mason's Daily Advertiser*. Endowed with his father's passion for reporting and living by his paper's motto, "The public will be our guide—the public good our end," Timothy's assertiveness (and intrusiveness) made him no stranger to controversy. Furthermore, knowing his responsibility to Charleston's public as a newsman, no one was going to tell him how best to do his job. Unfortunately, that is just what Colonel Jacob Read tried to do.

Almost immediately after launching his paper, Timothy found himself at odds with Read, a Charleston lawyer and former member of the Continental Congress. In the weeks prior, Colonel Read and a rival attorney, M. Cary (first name not printed), had quarreled over a court case involving seized maritime property. Harsh public postings naturally led to a scheduled duel between Read and Cary. However, not wishing to compound his troubles, Read sent a letter to Timothy asking him to keep the paper quiet on the matter, stating that while he was sympathetic to the First Amendment, the paper should butt out of private affairs. Making things worse for himself, Read ended his letter with a subtle threat, saying he would hold the editors responsible for any publicity given to his meeting with Cary.

Timothy was outraged and, as expected, obstinately refused the colonel's request. Upon rejection, Read lived up to his word and, despite his pending fight with Mr. Cary, challenged Timothy to a duel as well: "From the contemptible quarter it comes the scandal must be harmless with men who know me, but you having given it all the fling in your power by publishing it in your gazette, which must read where I am not known, 'tis to you I look for satisfaction."[46]

Timothy agreed to duel immediately after receiving the note but, in the meantime, unleashed the *Gazette*'s presses at Colonel Read's expense:

Alas my poor Jacob! Instead of this, we thought to have published his monody before his departure to that bourne whence no traveler returns. But still shifting with the varying wind he yet hopes to see better times. Poor fellow! None but the desperado can fight you. You should take yourself to another state—you there might strut about, you might wear a sword there, fit for your noble arm to wield. But where you are so well-known, words will not do. Fallen, fallen from his high estate, does he think that I, a weak mortal of 5 feet 6 inches, would attempt to raise him: No, my utmost exertings, will be to depress him 'till he shall be sufficiently humbled. No

advantages of high steps or bloody cudgels will I allow him; the protection
of the court shall be his security; he may there spout in safety.

With their duel set for the morning of June 27, 1794, Read and Timothy made their way toward the decided field, but authorities interrupted them just outside the city limits at King Street Road. It was the first of many frustrations the contest would encounter. In the second instance, Timothy recommended they fight on a sandbar in the Savannah River, to which Read replied he would not be heading that direction until October. Again, the two parties went back into negotiations.[47]

In all, Read and Timothy tried five separate times to carry out their affair, all of which were either called off or interrupted due to some asinine circumstance. Finally, after an extended period, the pair simply gave up trying to shoot each other and abandoned their duel altogether.

Perhaps a better example of an editors' duel actually coming to fruition was the Cunningham-Hatch affair of 1856. In the wake of Preston Brooks's beating of Charles Sumner on the House floor, *Evening News* editor John Cunningham and James Hatch, editor pro tem of the *Southern Standard*, entered into a series of heated exchanges using their own newspapers as vehicles for their personal tiffs. Hatch vehemently maintained that Cunningham's newspaper had taken a decidedly negative opinion of the Brooks-Sumner event by criticizing Brooks's actions as damaging to the state. Without hesitation, Hatch jumped at the opportunity to use his competitor's words to sell papers, leading his readers to believe that the *Evening News* had the gall to disagree with Sumner's attack and therefore did not have the state's best interests in mind. With the city hanging on every word, Hatch called out Cunningham publicly and accosted him repeatedly. Cunningham, of course, replied via his paper that Hatch was little more than a lying muckraker, informing him via a July 25 editorial that he was "not the responsible editor of the *Standard*" but instead a "recent-comer," calling out Hatch's northern birthplace of New Gloucester, Maine. From there, the fight was on.

Hatch and Cunningham eventually met at their prearranged dueling ground near the Charleston racecourse on July 28, 1856. After some preliminary haggling over positions and how best to hold their pistols, the two exchanged shots, but both missed badly. Deciding they had each proved their point, the two editors believed the matter settled and went back to work.[48]

Now, besides social order, a suitable ground was a crucial ingredient in any duel. In fact, once a man accepted a challenge from a worthy adversary, generally the first article discussed and agreed upon was a location where the duel could commence. Duelists—at least those with some respect for tradition—usually chose somewhere private or at least outside city limits to avoid an audience, an interruption or, worse, an arrest.

In New Orleans, for example, a city practically deadlocked with Charleston in terms of dueling incidences, the fabled spot for their affairs was an allée known simply as "The Oaks." Once part of a plantation owned by Jean Louis Allard in the 1770s, it is now the site of the public City Park. Today, the park holds the largest collection of mature live oaks in the country, including one of the original "dueling oaks," a marker of sorts for the fighting Creole's *affaires d'honneur*. Harriet Magruder's *A History of Louisiana* provides an excellent example of The Oaks' popularity as a dueling lane. Beneath these "cathedral aisles of nature" (as it was called by the *Times-Democrat* in 1892), it is written that as many as ten duels took place in 1839 all in the same afternoon. Moreover, dueling continued there until 1890—forty years after the property was converted to a public park.[49]

Charlestonians, for myriad reasons, never seemed to follow the habits of their Louisiana brethren—this in spite of the city holding the second-largest French population in the country during the eighteenth century. Whereas many duels fought in New Orleans were public, sometimes even referred to as festive events, their classical French pride was not virtuous among Charleston's locals. For them, strong traditions of English modesty prevented their airing of private matters. Christopher Gadsden and Robert Howe, for example, abandoned their first duel at Mazyck's pasture near the Liberty Tree in 1778 when, upon arriving, they found scores of rowdy spectators waiting for them.

Understandably, public witnesses to duels were a dangerous thing. At best, their presence on the field practically guaranteed a retelling of the duel to the newspapers. At worst, they cost lives. After Captain Holmes (first name not printed) and Gabriel Wall both missed each other during an exchange of shots in 1787, a few onlookers raucously hollered out their disappointment at the lack of bloodshed. Feeling egged on, the two reloaded and fired again. Wall was shot in the head and died instantly.[50]

Because Charlestonians never seemed to formally embrace one area over another as an official field or tract on which to carry out their duels, chosen grounds were usually random fields, riverbanks or beachheads. Areas north of town in the peninsula's "neck" area or somewhere outside modern-day Line Street were popular, as was the Washington Race Course, once part of Lowndes Plantation and now the site of Hampton Park near The Citadel.

Federal grounds were also preferable for their neutrality. That is, since places like Fort Johnson or Castle Pinckney were not state-governed areas, each was somewhat protected from local anti-dueling laws.[51]

Even though Philadelphia Alley (once known as Kinloch's Court, Cow Alley or Philadelphia Street) is frequently cited in dueling anecdotes, this secluded path between Cumberland and Queen Streets sorely lacks any hard evidence suggesting it was a preferred spot for inner-city dueling. Unfortunately, an unlikely swordfight involving General William Moultrie and an unnamed opponent appears to be the only duel popularly linked to this place, but primary sources on this particular battle are fleeting. In fact, when both the *News and Courier* and the *New York Times* printed the dubious tale as a history piece in 1894, there appeared no mention of the quarrel's cause or the approximate year as to when the fight supposedly took place—if it even did.[52]

Another sometimes-favored dueling lane was a patch of land once located near modern-day Magnolia Cemetery owned by a Charleston-area social society known as the Oaks Club, (not to be confused with The Oaks of New Orleans or the Oaks Club of Goose Creek). Members of this club privately owned the land as a co-op of sorts and all too often made the area readily available for dueling purposes. Because of the compound-type nature of the real estate, many duelists (some of whom were members) could freely carry out their challenges away from the prying eyes of public authorities.

Traveling farther, mostly deserted barrier islands such as nearby Long Island (now Isle of Palms), Dewees Island or Cumberland and Tybee Islands off the Georgia coast were desirous. One particular area on Edisto Island once known as "The Sands" certainly hosted its share of duels in the eighteenth century.[53]

Not surprisingly, duelists wishing for total, practically guaranteed anonymity often ventured far out of town and even beyond state lines. Various sandbanks on the Savannah River, for example, constantly served as venues on which to settle scores. The reason for this extensive travel was threefold. First, any witness to the duel, accidental or not, would likely not know the combatants on sight, thus further ensuring their duel's confidentiality. Second, a secluded environment protected the loser from public scorn and embarrassment (assuming he survived, of course). Finally, a state's authority over riverbanks and sandbars was notoriously confusing. The ever-changing river waters constantly altered the overall landscape year after year, making jurisdiction all the more difficult for law enforcement.[54]

The large oak trees that still stand in the intersection of Congress Street and Parkwood Avenue near Hampton Park and the former site of the Washington Race Course mark the location where Edward Magrath killed William Taber in their 1856 duel. *Courtesy of the Charleston Museum.*

Chapter 4

THE WRITTEN WORD

Mandates, Manuals and Mr. Wilson

In colonial America and assorted regions throughout Western Europe, dueling with pistols was a major issue, and by the 1760s, the custom had certainly graduated from archaic lances, halberds and broad swords. Eventually though, duelists everywhere needed some sort of order within the rite. Although most participants generally understood proper forms for dueling etiquette, the evolution of pistol use within it threatened to run roughshod over society, turning otherwise gentlemanly affairs into bloody carnage.

A major turning point in terms of modern dueling came with the Irish-written *Code Duello*, published in 1777 under the Clonmel Summer Assizes. This short manual listed a firm yet interpretable set of rules and detailed every aspect of a duel among gentlemen. The *Duello* kept its descriptions brief but still managed to include honorable protocols, including proper times in which challenges could be delivered and received, the specific roles of appointed assistants (or "seconds"), how many shots could (or should) be fired and how many wounds could be received before satisfaction was properly attained.

If nothing else, these new standards ensured that all efforts toward a noncombative resolution had been exhausted and that violence was the only remaining suitable course of action for the two at odds. Also understanding that death could result from such activity, the *Duello* established rather progressive attempts to limit physical harm to each opponent by restricting the terms of the engagement, providing medical care and calling for a set number of witnesses who could attest to a duel's fairness and provide legal testimony if necessary. Finally—and maybe most importantly—the *Code Duello*'s publication ably prevented personal vendettas among individuals, entire families and special-interest groups.

Before this time, there were other rulebooks and printed guides in existence. For example, two works written under the Italian codes were the *Flos Duellatorum* (or *The Flower of Battle*), written circa 1410, and *Il Duello* from around 1550. Each in its own right was a thorough training guide for all forms of singular combat against an opponent. Popular as these books were in their day, however, medieval combat tactics as a whole were effectively useless by the seventeenth century. Advancements in weapons technology and the advent of firearms rendered both obsolete. Pistols were by now the only essential tools necessary for a duel, and the *Code Duello* at last formally accepted the use of them.

Besides the *Code Duello*, there were at least a couple of casual British attempts to revise the *Duello*. In 1824, for example, London publishers Knight and Lacey released *The British Code of Duel: A Reference to the Laws and Honour and the Character of Gentlemen*. A few years later, *The Only Approved Guide through All the Stages of a Quarrel* by Joseph Hamilton appeared in 1829. Despite these works, post-Revolutionary Americans still wished themselves separate from their British forebears, and most local elites cared little for English codes of conduct when taking the field of honor. Thus, neither publication was well received in Charleston; each was regarded as a wordy rewrite of the old eighteenth-century codes. In fact, Hamilton's book does a far better job of preaching against dueling than making suggestions for its proper use, clearly proclaiming in his opening paragraph:

> *The advocates for the custom allege in its defence* [sic], *that it places gentlemen on an equal footing; and that according to the prevailing notions of worldly honor, a challenge cannot be refused, nor an insult overlooked. Not one of those, I believe, has ventured to assert that it is consistent with either law, morality, or religion; but that it is contrary to all those three, as well as to common sense and real honor, has been alleged by numbers.*[55]

Also, an anonymously written, eighty-four-page guidebook entitled *The Art of Dueling* appeared in 1836 and provided recommendations for young duelists, including proper settlements to arguments, practice methods, firing tactics and even a chapter offering precautions. But like its predecessors, it held fast to flowery European tastes mostly unappealing to American southerners.

To be sure, the sheer number of duels carried out among Charlestonians and southerners alike grew rapidly as the nineteenth century wore on. Adding to the widespread arguing were the severe political calamities of the 1820s and '30s. The grossly unpopular Tariff of 1824, the "Tariff of Abominations" in 1828 and the ultimate Nullification Crisis in 1832 all resulted in untold numbers of challenges passing between political opponents. Priorities were questioned. Characters were scorned. Insults flew.

Finally, genuinely concerned for the citizens of his state, Governor John Lyde Wilson took it upon himself to revise the antiquated ways of the *Code Duello* and write his own recommendations for South Carolina's undisciplined duelists. In 1838, Wilson published *The Code of Honor: Or Rules for the Government of Principals and Seconds in Dueling.* The book quickly became the most revered manual of its day in the South, and, as far as southerners were concerned, it was a masterpiece of its time.

John Lyde Wilson was born in 1784 near Bennettsville in Marlboro County, just south of the North Carolina border. A practicing attorney in Georgetown, he served three separate terms as a state congressional representative in 1806, 1812 and 1816. In 1818, Wilson served in the state senate and became governor in 1822, serving two years before returning to his senate seat in 1826. Some years later, he served as a Charleston delegate to the Nullification Convention of 1833, where he voiced his stern support for South Carolina's right to self-government.

To his credit, Wilson was vitally interested in all manner of public affairs in and around the Lowcountry—some of which were not resolved peacefully. In the summer of 1835, for example, Wilson was an active participant in the tarring and feathering of a local barber named Richard Wood, a suspected trafficker of goods stolen from Charleston homes and nearby plantations. Under Wilson's supervision, Wood was

> *immediately marched down to Price's Wharf, tied to a post and there he received twenty lashes on his bare back. A tub of tar was then emptied upon his head in such a way as to cause it to extend over his whole body, and the miscreant barber was decorated with a covering of loose cotton, the principle material in which he had carried on his illicit traffic.*[56]

Wilson's intimate knowledge of controlled dueling and its history was through more than just quiet study. He held firsthand experience in the tradition, as he was a witness to several duels throughout his younger years and reportedly participated in at least one. Aside from his personal

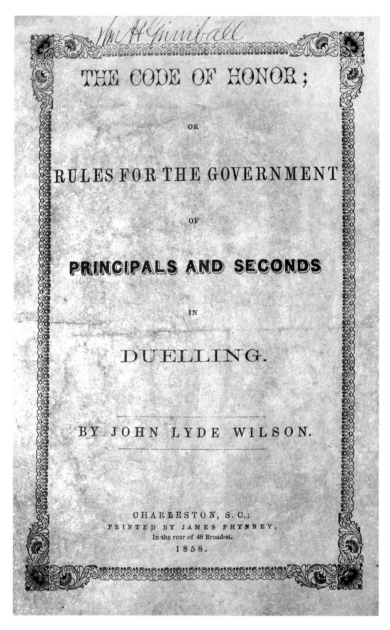

The front cover of John Lyde Wilson's manual, *The Code of Honor*, reprinted by Charleston printer James Phynney on Broad Street. Although it was originally released in 1838, Wilson's death eventually prompted a reprint in 1858. *Courtesy of the Charleston Museum.*

experiences with dueling, family connections in fact bound him to the deadly tradition. As it turned out, both Wilson's first and second marriages forever linked him to the most famous duel in American history. On New Year's Eve 1809, he wed Charlotte Alston, sister-in-law to Aaron Burr's daughter Theodosia. After Charlotte's premature death in 1817, Wilson married Rebecca Eden, a former ward of Aaron Burr, on October 17, 1825. [57]

Above all, Wilson was a master of *strategic* dueling but not necessarily from a sharpshooter's point of view. Instead, his real genius rested in the negotiation and planning stages. A natural-born politician, Wilson had a knack—nigh a gift—for filibustering and convoluting an argument so well that his dueling challenges ostensibly became battles of attrition. His quarrel with Henry Middleton perhaps best exemplifies his dueling prowess and cunning.

On February 27, 1824, while attending a reception hosted by Charleston's St. Cecilia Society, Wilson stepped on the toes of the wrong man—literally. While asking a seated woman for a dance, Wilson overstepped his bow, landing his foot atop that of Henry Middleton. Viewing Wilson's misstep as a physical attack, Middleton confronted the former governor, which kicked off an intense argument ripe with insults and foul language. By the end of the row, Wilson had essentially promised Middleton that he would be receiving a challenge as soon as the next morning. But exploiting his opponent's well-known temper and impatience, Wilson waited more than two weeks until March 14 before sending a note. Enraged at Wilson's tardiness, and considering the delay an added insult, Middleton quickly put forth Fort Johnson as his choice of ground and that the two should fire pistols a mere three paces apart. Wilson replied that fighting at so close a distance was "unwarrantable" and roundly rejected the proposal.[58]

Wilson and Middleton's back-and-forth arbitrations continued for weeks, and at every turn, Middleton played right into Wilson's hands. With each proposal Middleton sent, Wilson cleverly answered by consistently (and intentionally) putting forth complicated counteroffers and adjusted stipulations for the duel's time, place and attendees—all of which were physically impossible for Middleton to meet. For example, at one point Middleton tendered that he "would meet Mr. Wilson at any place other than the neighborhood Georgetown" to carry out their duel. Wilson quickly offered to fight Middleton at Georgetown Fort, which he now knew was too close to Middleton's home. Obviously wishing to avoid trouble with family members, Middleton had no choice but to refuse. In another instance, Middleton angrily put forth to Wilson that he was ready to fight any time in the next week except for Friday. Wilson politely replied that he was busy most of those days, but Friday would be fine. A flabbergasted Middleton again had no alternative but to decline.[59]

By the end of March 1824, Wilson attained his goal of frustrating Middleton to the point where he just stopped trying. The whole dilemma quickly faded, and the proposed duel passed silently into permanent limbo—just as Wilson had intended. Writing in the March 30, 1824 edition of the *City Gazette*, Wilson put an end to the whole matter, stating, "I take my leave of the public, with regret that it became necessary to say a single word upon a subject where individuals only are concerned."

So with all his duelistic professionalism, who better than to pen dueling's ultimate instruction manual? Of course, Governor Wilson's new codes followed a few core principles listed in the *Code Duello*, including the essential uses for seconds and surgeons, but that's where the similarities ended. Wilson's new rules for an honorable duel were specific, paying astute attention to every detail, unlike the former, open-minded *Duello*.

In fact, at the time of his publication, Wilson claimed that he had neither read nor consulted the *Duello* since it was a product of Europe and thus irrelevant to the character and honor of gentlemen within South Carolina. Whether he was speaking truthfully remains dubious since he more than once referenced specific rules in it, calling them "old notions." For example, under the *Code Duello*, rules sixteen and seventeen gave the challenged party his choice of weapon, location and distance apart. Wilson decided this was insignificant, if not ridiculous. He insisted instead that "each party is entitled to perfect equality" and continued in chapter three:

> *The old notion that the party challenged, was authorized to name the time, place, distance and weapon, has long been exploded; nor would a man of chivalric honor use such a right, if he possessed it. The time must be as soon as practicable, the place such as had ordinarily been used where the parties are, the distance usual, and the weapon that which is most generally used, which, in this state, is the pistol.[60]*

Furthermore, Wilson was diligent in discussing the delicate administration and delivery of the all-important challenge. Formerly, the *Duello* had decreed that challenges were to be written out on paper and hand delivered during daylight hours. Wilson did not stem from this but further specified and elaborated on the recommendation that a challenge to duel be the absolute *last* resort. Wilson, moreover, made a point that duelists should never jump to conclusions since snap decisions could result in uncivilized and uncalled-for barbarism. As he explains in his very first chapter, parties should "never send a challenge in the first instance, for that precludes all negotiation."[61]

When it came to actually issuing a written challenge, duelists as a whole were careful not to specifically mention pistols or seconds or even use the word "duel." They were gentlemen, after all, and in so being, most of their notes tended to dance around the delicate subject of killing each other. Besides, to mention a duel on paper could present incriminating evidence of foul play. For example, when Edward Magrath sent his challenge to William R. Taber on Broad Street, he wished only to "demand the satisfaction recognized in such cases. I invite you serially to a meeting and refer you for the necessary arrangements to my friend, James Conner, esq. who will hand you this. I am your obedient servant." Thus, just like Magrath's language here, many challenges were vague and detail-less. The whole point was to agree to fight first and iron out the niceties later.[62]

Obviously, it must be noted that whatever manual or instruction book on dueling—be it the *Flos Duellatorum*, *Code Duello*, *The Art of Dueling* or even Governor Wilson's eight-chapter opus—was at its heart nothing more than a mere listing of non-enforceable recommendations. In the end, it was all up to the duelists and their seconds to hash out what their specific procedures and needs were going to be and how they were going to carry them out. Many, to their credit, did at least a somewhat decent job of sticking to the civilized principles of honorable combat put forth by the available literature of the day. Unsurprisingly though, Charleston's elite were a dogged group, and numerous heated debates consistently erupted among politicos, socialites, dilettantes and otherwise bitter enemies of which no written word could suffice. In these extreme cases, only a bloody and absolute defeat would bring about satisfaction. Written codes be damned.

In such instances, the *Code Duello* and Governor Wilson both acknowledged the fact that some arguments were indeed fiercer than others. For instance, in severe situations like extra harsh insults or physical assault, each allowed special amendments that permitted more serious fighting. Rule 24 of the *Duello* noted that "slight cases" involving cruel offenses could permit the use of two pistols instead of one, each loaded, charged and ready to fire. Governor Wilson conversely backed off a bit when it came to duelists using more than one pistol. That is, his rules did not directly speak for or against using multiple weapons in a single duel but instead chose to let the severity of the argument dictate the ultimate nature of the gunfight—something the adversaries and their seconds would have to hash out for themselves.

He writes in chapter eight, "Can every insult be compromised is a mooted and vexed question. On this subject no rules can be given that will be satisfactory."[63]

A duel fought at the Four-Mile House outside Charleston in 1794 is an example of such ferocity. Unfortunately, the causes of the challenge from Mr. James Mitchell to Mr. Sterling (first name not printed) are still unknown. It is also unknown if either consulted the guidelines of the *Code Duello*, although judging from the unforgiving terms of their duel, they likely didn't. Thankfully, however, Mitchell's second, Richard Gough, published his eyewitness account of the contest in the August 1 edition of the *South Carolina State-Gazette*. After some light negotiating among Mitchell, Sterling and their attending seconds, it was decided that the two combatants would hold two pistols—one in each hand—and position themselves some forty feet apart. Once given the word to begin, Mitchell and Sterling were to walk toward each other while firing at will. Whoever had the last shot then (assuming the contest progressed to this point) was to approach his opponent, stick the pistol to his chest, squeeze the trigger "and kill him if he pleased."

Gough continues, "They accordingly marched up within about six or seven yards of each other and fired almost at the same time; they then advanced a little further and Mr. M. fired his other pistol with his left hand and missed… Accordingly, Mr. S. put his pistol to Mr. M.'s breast." Graciously, Sterling did not fire point-blank into Mitchell. Instead, he pulled the gun away and discharged his gun into the air. Afterward, as the *Gazette* concludes, the two joined each other for breakfast and remained friends thereafter.[64]

Now, attacks to a man's moral fiber may be one thing, but slander toward his woman was something else entirely. In fact, duels fought over the defamation of a woman were popularly considered more serious in nature than any fought over politics, property or morality. Essentially, if a man dared insult a female, all bets were off, and he was in a great deal of trouble. Defamation to females in the eighteenth century was deemed so serious that even the *Code Duello* addressed it. As article ten states: "Any insult to a lady under a gentleman's care or protection is to be considered as, by one degree, a greater offense than if given to the gentleman personally, and the contest is to be regulated accordingly."

Alas, Charleston men getting into trouble with women was a relatively common event. Case in point was the near-death experience of Captain George Izard, son of College of Charleston co-founder Ralph Izard, who was engaged to a Miss Pierre (first name not printed), a French refugee from Santo Domingo's slave insurrection in the 1790s. Whether because of his military career or just cold feet, Izard for whatever reason continually refused to marry the young woman, constantly delaying their wedding date over the course of several years. Worse still was a letter from Izard's sister describing Miss Pierre "as having a *nez-retrousse*" (or snubbed nose).[65]

Deciding his sister insulted over Izard's delays and his sibling's mockery, Miss Pierre's brother intervened, traveling all the way to Fort Mifflin in Philadelphia to challenge the general to a duel. The two soon faced off somewhere in New Jersey near the banks of the Delaware River. Because of the offense to a female, the two agreed to fire not one but two shots each before satisfaction could be granted. Upon the second volley, Izard received serious wounds to both his right arm and chest. He later wrote in his memoirs how surprised he was not just to have survived the duel but to be "relieved from all further engagement of marriage" to Miss Pierre.[66]

Indeed, insulting a woman was bad. Much worse, however, was carrying on inappropriate relations with a married one. Offenses such as this were hardly ever forgiven and most simply by their nature were expected to end in a duel. John Rutledge Jr., whose father signed the United Sates Constitution and whose uncle, Edward, was the youngest signer of the Declaration of Independence, killed Dr. Horatio Senter in just such a lovelorn duel fought on January 19, 1804.

In 1792, Rutledge married Sarah Motte Smith, daughter of the esteemed Right Reverend Robert Smith, rector of St. Philip's Church in Charleston and a wealthy landowner. Despite a seemingly happy marriage—one that produced six children—Sarah fell for Horatio Senter (listed as "Horace" in Savannah's mortuary records), a physician from Newport, Rhode Island. The two met while in Connecticut, where Sarah and her family were spending the summer in 1803 away from the Lowcountry heat and its malaria-riddled rice plantations. Smitten, Dr. Senter traveled to Charleston later that year and even called on Sarah at her father's home, Brabant Plantation.[67]

Naturally, it was only a matter of time before John Rutledge discovered the scandalous affair. Infuriated and humiliated, Rutledge attacked Senter in the front hallway at Brabant and immediately challenged him. Taking the field in Savannah, Rutledge shot Senter in the leg. The wound festered for several days before lockjaw set in. On January 14, 1804, Senter died.[68]

Chapter 5

SECONDS COUNT

Composure amongst Carnage

O ut of the entire list of terms defined within the *Code Duello*, it is interesting that the actual firing of guns is not earnestly addressed until rule nineteen. That means, of course, the first eighteen requisites spoke primarily to the duel's fragile management tasks and overall preparation. This delay is by intentional design. A common misperception still existing even in today's time is a duel's exact execution. There are still numerous false assumptions that once a challenge was put forth, the two arguers immediately went out somewhere, drew their pistols and fired away on one another until someone died.

In truth, no traditionalistic duelist worth his salt would agree to this kind of haphazard gun slinging. Impromptu showdowns may look good on twentieth-century movie screens, but they were completely unacceptable among landed gentlemen—usually. For a proper duel to move forward required tremendous legwork and was, in fact, quite necessary for both sides if they hoped to preserve their honor. Fortunately, by virtue of discipline, plenty of duels ended peacefully thanks to the lengthy processes of carrying one out, some taking months or even more than a year before coming to fruition.

Playing a major role in all these arrangements and arbitrations was the second. So what exactly was a second? First recorded in the sixteenth century, a second was as much a participant in a duel as the triggerman himself, and any person even thinking of dueling needed to appoint one before a challenge could be issued. Governor John Lyde Wilson for one knew the vital importance of seconds and acknowledged that one of the main reasons for his 1838 publication was for their benefit. To him, an inexperienced second was a sure liability, as he wrote in his introduction: "I believe that nine duels out of ten, if not ninety-nine out of a hundred, originate in the want of experienced seconds. A book of authority, to which they can refer in matters where they are uninformed, will therefore be a desideratum."[69]

Simply put, a second was a volunteer arbiter of sorts, a kind of secretary or personal assistant to the challenged or challenging duelist. If nothing else, he was hopefully a man with a cool head, a slightly more neutral involvement in the whole affair and was capable of soothing the emotional wounds of his boss. Moreover, seconds needed to be reliable friends or at least colleagues who could be called upon to do the bidding of the duelist. As part of rule fourteen of the *Code Duello* noted, "Seconds are to be of equal in society with the principals they attend." Thus, to assume a second's position, one had to be on the same social, economic and educative ground as the combatant. Paid employees, children, lower-class workers, slaves and spouses generally were prohibited from serving as seconds.[70]

Above all, seconds served as chief liaisons between rival parties and as such carried out dozens of duties on their principals' behalf. Deliverance of communiqués—especially the written challenges—was a priority. Through this mediation, of course, a good second could successfully prolong an affair to a point where neither combatant could deal with the stress of facing injury or death and, consequently, call the whole thing off. If that particular mission should fail though, seconds were then responsible for arbitrating the actual duel and helping ensure a fair fight. Seconds negotiated everything on their principals' behalf, including times, places and whose or what kind of weapons were to be employed.

While the *Code Duello* only sporadically notes the assorted duties of the second, Governor John Lyde Wilson's 1838 codes dedicated a serious number of pages to them, greatly expanding on the *Duello*'s somewhat nonchalance. The *Duello*'s rule twenty-one, for example, stated, "Seconds are bound to attempt reconciliation before the meeting takes place." This, according to Wilson, was incredibly insufficient, and he addressed would-be seconds directly:

> *You are supposed to be cool and collected, and your friend's feelings are more or less irritated. Use every effort to soothe and tranquilize your principal; do not see things in the same aggravated light in which he views them. Extenuate the conduct of his adversary whenever you see clearly an opportunity to do so,*

without doing violence to your friend's irritated mind. Endeavor to persuade him that there must have been some misunderstanding in the matter. Check him if he uses opprobrious epithet towards his adversary, and never permit improper or insulting words in the note(s) you carry.[71]

While a second's duties were indeed numerous, at least his mission was simple enough: keep the two aggravated individuals away from each other as long as possible, thereby giving them time to think things through, hopefully cool off a bit and ultimately just let bygones be bygones. Wilson again stressed that a good duelist should be willing to put the entire matter in the hands of his second, essentially placing his life in this friend's care. To their credit, seconds usually performed nobly. Colonel Francis Kinloch Huger of Charleston, for example, likely saved the lives of Francis Quash and Thomas G. Simons in 1826. In the midst of their duel, Huger put forth a masterful letter explaining to both: "Affairs of this nature are usually magnified by rumor, frequently repeated, and commented upon by officious friends and silly acquaintances, until they assume a false appearance, and bitter and resentful feelings are excited which never originally existed. The affair… does not impeach your principles as gentlemen, or your courage as men."[72]

Huger's words delivered the desired, calming effect. In response, Quash wrote, "I regret the misunderstanding and affray which occurred between Mr. Tho. G. Simons and myself. It did not arise on my part from any deliberate intention to injure or offend." Simons cancelled the duel immediately thereafter.[73]

Expectedly, for all the good seconds, alas, there were some bad ones. Charleston's J. Davidson Legare, for example, acting on poor advice from his friend-turned-second Mr. M.N. Waring, entered into a duel with John Dunovant on August 2, 1853, the result of a conversation the two had concerning a Columbia woman. Egged on by several friends (including Waring), Legare issued a challenge to Dunovant, writing, "Give me that redress which wounded and injured honor has a right to demand at your hands."[74]

Before the duel, Waring assured Legare that his opponent was clueless in the ways of a gun. This notion only added to Legare's self-confidence since his friends had always revered him a crack shot. Thus, feeling practically guaranteed of vindication, Legare met Dunovant near the old racecourse just north of town. The *Charleston Courier* announced the following morning: "A duel was fought in the vicinity of the city early yesterday morning, between John Dunovant, Esq. of Chester, and J.D. Legare, Esq. of this city, in which we regret to state, the latter was killed at the first fire."

For any duelist, having a calm and levelheaded second was surely a tremendous asset. For the second, however, his was an inherently dangerous task. Worst of all, certain specific conditions existed within both the *Duello* and Wilson's codes that if agreements could not be reached between seconds, each was allowed to post the other, issue their own challenges and, if needs be, shoot it out among themselves. Thus, a careless or overly biased second could easily end up fighting his own duel if he wasn't careful.

Finally, the second was in the most danger when it came time for the actual firing of shots. Foremost, the seconds were in charge of loading their respective principals' pistols. Both the *Duello* and Wilson urged that all weaponry be handled exclusively by the seconds right up until the combatants were in position. Rule eighteen of the *Code Duello* stated, "The seconds load in the presence of each other unless they give their mutual honors that they have charged smoothe [*sic*] and single, which should be held sufficient." Governor Wilson moreover elaborated on this initial standard, writing in chapter seven, "Each second informs the other when he is about to load, and invites his presence, but the seconds rarely attend in such invitation, as gentlemen may be safely trusted in the matter."[75]

Unfortunately, one is quick to notice that both the *Duello* and Wilson's code do not *enforce* any secondary witnessing of the loading process. Therefore, seconds were allowed complete, unsupervised control of their principals' pistols based on nothing more than the character and trust of a gentleman. This somewhat careless omission left the door wide open.

Enter the cheater.

Short of saying it *never* happened, cheating among duelists and seconds was rare. As with many things, there were degrees to which duelists could stretch the rules of decency. Traditionalists wholly denounced combatants arriving at the field wearing baggy clothes, overcoats or cloaks that clouded their profiles—even though such garments were not illegal per se.

Additionally, neither the 1777 *Code Duello* nor Wilson's 1832 revised codes accepted or denied the use of spectacles, but the wearing of them was dubious. Naturally, to deny an opponent the use of his glasses was certainly unsportsmanlike if not blatantly rude, and if he required them in daily life, he should have them on the field as well. Of course, if he were to show up wearing his glasses, the lenses therein were expected to be of non-tinted, clear glass. Use of shooting glasses was typically discreditable to most, although arguments for and against them sometimes arose depending on the choice of ground. Colored lenses with narrowed fields of vision cut down glare, especially if dueling on a beach or riverbank late in the day, but

Shooter's glasses, circa 1850. Reserved for sporting purposes, darkened amber-tinted glass cut down on glare, while the narrowed fields of vision in each lens helped with aim. *Courtesy of the Charleston Museum.*

in truth, the advantages of these specialized pieces were perceived as just a bit too far over the lines of courtesy.

Way past questionable attire though was the use of altered pistols and false bullets. This type of deceit was downright corrupt, if not just plain evil, and a user of such could expect nothing less than public derision wherever he went (assuming, that is, his deviance was discovered). Thankfully, there have not yet emerged any recorded instances of cheating duelists in Charleston— although some have come awfully close.

One such pair of pistols surviving today in a South Carolina family's private collection appears to have been customized for just such a reason. At first glance, the barrel interior at both muzzles is smoothbore—a typical requirement for dueling pistols. Thus, any second looking down the barrel under normal sunlight would not see the rifled grooves that begin about halfway down the bore in one of the pieces. A deliberate and deceitful modification to be sure, secretly intended to make one pistol more accurate than the other.[76]

Furthermore, a cased set of matching pistols in the collections of the Charleston Museum is equipped with a compartment for storing bullets. However, mixed in with the lead slugs are ones made from pressed charcoal,

Except for weight, a faux charcoal bullet (left) is nearly indiscernible from a genuine lead bullet (right). A careless second would not notice the difference and thus could load the wrong one in his principal's gun. Both real and fake bullets were found housed within a cased pair of pistols belonging to a Charlestonian in the 1840s. *Courtesy of the Charleston Museum.*

which would disintegrate upon ignition. A conniving second would know the difference in weight between the two projectiles and choose a genuine lead ball (all the while hoping the opposing second would choose a false one).

Besides making sure his principal's pistol was going to work, a second was responsible for giving the word to fire, as well as calling a halt. Naturally, any mistake—or even an appearance of one—during this critical time could be interpreted as an attempt to gain an advantage. Thus, an otherwise civilized duel could quickly turn into a chaotic, deadly situation. Wilson was clear in instructing seconds how best to handle wrongdoers while in the field. He asserts in chapter five, "Each second has a loaded pistol (on his person) to enforce a fair combat according to the rules agreed on; and if a principal fires before the word or time agreed on, he is at liberty to fire at him, and if such second's principal fall, it is his duty to do so."[77]

On the afternoon of September 29, 1812, twenty-two-year-old William Bay fought a duel with his political rival, twenty-one-year-old William Thomas Crafts, over what was described as "a mere trifle." At some point over a previous dinner conversation, Crafts had suggested to Bay that the Republican Party (the same of which Bay was an ardent supporter) was one suited more for lesser men without any sense. Upon this declaration, the conversation spiraled into an intense argument. Finally, after some terse bickering, Crafts loudly proclaimed that one of the current Republican constituents of Virginia, John Randolph of Roanoke, was "just such another tall, ugly, gawky Yankee-looking fellow" as Bay was. Having had more than enough, Bay threw a punch at Crafts, and a challenge to duel soon followed.[78]

Accompanied by their seconds, the opponents met on a field near Charleston's racecourse. What happened next remains unclear, but more than one account of the duel suggests that Crafts fired before his second gave the word to do so. Bay never had a chance. Crafts's shot struck him in the chest. A witness wrote, "The ball penetrated the heart of Bay [and] he expired in a few seconds without uttering a groan." Bay's second, certainly well aware of the attitudes reserved for cheaters, was said to have been "frantic at the idea that he did not shoot Crafts and kill him upon the spot for [his] violation of the rule."[79]

Of course, strong egos could (and often did) pollute many duels, thus diminishing the role of the second to a mere go-between subject to the whims of his boss. For instance, a most unusual, albeit complicated, quarrel erupted in Charleston in the spring of 1823. Although the root of the argument was never printed, so heated was the bickering that by June of that year, Benjamin Allston was set to fight two consecutive duels against Drs. Charles Atkins *and* Edward Cuthbert. From the get-go, there were harsh disagreements among the seconds as to the terms of the duel. In one instance even, the three seconds almost dueled because of arguments over how to fight the one that they were officiating. Eventually, it became clear that all involved were interested in bloodshed only.

At first, everything seemed normal. Seconds to the three parties followed their respective protocols. Atkins and Cuthbert, however, in a show of force demanded their seconds abandon all conventional thinking and propose to Allston that each principal fire at a measly five paces apart. Incensed at their boldness, Allston refused. Atkins and Cuthbert, unfazed by Allston's common sense, conjured up an even more ridiculous counteroffer. Instead of the same old boring duel of marksmanship, they demanded their seconds put forth a test of nerves.

Sloughing off their seconds' vehement objections, the duelists would have to agree to one of the following procedures: either stand back to back and, within five paces, quickly wheel around and fire; or face off at two paces with pistols positioned on the ground and, at the word, scoop them up and fire away. Allston published his response to Cuthbert via the June 13 edition of the *Southern Patriot and Commercial Advertiser*: "Considering this a glaring and palpable absurdity, I unhesitatingly rejected it, as it was evidently obvious, that no man could efficiently use weapons in this manner without the greatest skill, and knowing that Dr. Atkins and yourself had never so practiced, that inequality was evident."

Relentlessly, Atkins and Cuthbert again suggested a farcical contest, the terms of which appeared a few days later via the same paper:

> *Stipulations for a Duel, to take place at Fort Johnson…*
> *1st. The time of meeting—the hour of 11 o'clock on Wednesday*
> *2nd. The distance—Five paces shall be the distance.*
> *3rd. The manner of fighting—The parties shall have two pistols. The one in the right hand cocked, and the trigger sprung. The one in the left hand half-cocked and the trigger unsprung. Both pistols shall be discharged [at] the word fire.*

Once again, Allston refused. Finally, some weeks later, seconds to all three parties mercifully, albeit barely, negotiated a truce and permanently suspended all negotiations.

Obviously, the entire series of events within the Allston-Atkins-Cuthbert affair made for a dishonorable farce. If nothing else, the threesome succeeded in turning a respectable duel into little more than a bigheaded circus act. Likely influenced by this very duel, in fact, Governor Wilson addressed the subject of insubordinate duelists not listening to their seconds by stating, "When your principal refuses to do what you require of him, decline further acting on that ground, and inform the opposing second of your withdrawal from the negotiation."[80]

One final example of seconds-gone-stupid is the death of Arthur Alfred Gilling of Edisto Island, a man of strong conviction—and a locally renowned sharpshooter. He was so sure of himself, in fact, that upon challenging one Mr. Bailey (first name not printed), a political adversary from Edingsville,

Arthur Alfred Gilling's box tomb (foreground; sometimes called a chest tomb or box grave) sits near the northwest corner of the Presbyterian Church on Edisto Island. *Author's photo.*

Gilling instructed his second to allow Bailey's side to go ahead and make any and all decisions as to time, place and weapons and to furthermore assure them that whatever their terms, they would be agreed upon.

Unlike his opponent, Bailey was coy and altogether unfamiliar in the ways of a gun. However, unwilling to doom his burgeoning political career by backing down from a challenge, he agreed to fight Gilling at The Sands near Edingsville on February 12, 1839. Because of Gilling's unmatched dueling prowess, seconds for both sides firmly believed at the time that Bailey had practically no chance of survival and even jested about it between themselves in the minutes prior to the duel. Further placing his personal vote of no confidence in his friend, Bailey's own second arrived with a gift for his principal: a small mattress with which he and the accompanying surgeon could more easily carry away Bailey's body.[81]

Once Bailey and Gilling assumed their positions, their seconds presented them their pistols. Bailey's second bid him goodbye, stepped away and then gave the word to fire.

While Arthur Alfred Gilling may have been well prepared to duel that day, he was likely *not* prepared to die. Unfortunately for him, that is exactly what happened after Bailey's bullet pierced his skull. Fittingly, Bailey paid all the costs for Gilling's funeral and subsequent burial at the Presbyterian Church on Edisto Island, even adding his own personal touch at the end of the tombstone's inscription: "Prepare to Meet Thy God."[82]

Chapter 6

ARMED AND DANGEROUS

Weaponry for the Would-Be Duelist

For most Europeans, dueling with pistols was a tragic disgrace, and those who used them were often denounced as barbarous, lazy and clumsy. After all, any buffoon or drunken idiot could point and fire a gun at someone and (with a little luck) kill him outright. Thus, for refined European duelists, firearms of any sort were meager tools only, reserved for cheaters and vagabonds, beggars and thieves.

To their credit, swordsmanship was an integral part of any young European lad's education and was, to an extent, incorporated into their social training as late as the Victorian period. In fact, perhaps harkening back to their British ancestry even after Charleston's newfound independence were a few locals who operated fencing schools around the turn of the nineteenth century. Captain John Oliver, for instance, hosted fencing tutorials at the Republican Coffeehouse on Tradd Street once a week in 1795; a 1799 newspaper advertisement announced "The Fencing Academy for Broad and Small Swords," which met on Meeting Street at Heyligar's Tavern; and Augustus de Graffe employed a sword-fighting room within Vaux Hall Garden on Queen Street in 1800.[83]

Of course, to fight with a blade took balance, quickness and agility, not to mention a terrific degree of athleticism. Unfortunately, many in Charleston saw it as a learned skill, a mere sport not suitable for affairs of honor. For them, pistols were just better tools for the job, and by the early 1700s, traditional duels once employing blades began undertaking a more murderous turn to gunplay. Thus, the duelists' use of firearms came to underscore Americanized dueling.

Charlestonians cared little for the views of their foreign counterparts. Here, firearms balanced the scales by effectively removing talent and skill from the equation and rolling out the welcome mat for just about anyone who wished to take the field. Moreover, shooting at someone—as many southerners truly believed—was an undeniably quick and thorough settlement to arguable affairs. So what if someone bloodied up another with a blade? He would likely survive and, what's worse, live to insult again. Therefore—in Charleston anyway—the bang of a pistol did a far better job of concluding things than did the swipe of a sword, and as a result, cased pairs of precision-matched dueling pistols became fashionable accoutrements among Charleston gentlemen.

The dueling pistol, as it is referred to historically, was not a specific firearm form. Even into the mid-1700s, after pistol dueling emerged as more or less acceptable, local gunsmiths hesitated to officially make (much less market) any handgun and call it a dueling pistol for fear of alienating their anti-duelist customers or by aiding and abetting deadly violence. In reality, after the publication of the *Code Duello*, just about any large-sized pistol could pass among the elites as a firearm suitable for a duelist. By the early federal period, Charleston gunsmith shops like John Milner's of Snitter's Ally (once near Church Street), Jacob Buckham's on Queen Street and Anthony Derverneys's on Broad Street were all making and selling singular large-bore and long-barreled pistols as well as cased pairs but advertising them usually as "target" or "sporting" pieces.[84]

Prior to 1790, most pistols preferred by duelists were of a larger caliber, usually falling somewhere between .577 and .60; were not always equipped with a foresight; and possessed a simple grooved notch at the breech to serve as a rear sight. Although considered today as "duelers," these guns were in effect general-purpose weapons adaptable for use militarily and otherwise.[85]

After the turn of the nineteenth century, a duelist's choice for a proper handgun still matched the *Duello*'s ideals of half-inch (or so) bore and a nine- to ten-inch barrel length, but by then, further adjustments and custom additions were included. In a push for increased precision, gunsmiths added spurred trigger guards, which provided an ancillary rest for the middle finger of the gun hand, further improving a duelist's grip while in an outreached, aiming position. Gun makers also began adding or retrofitting thicker and stronger octagonal barrels to replace the weaker round ones. Even though these thicker barrels made for heavier weapons, the added strength helped increase accuracy.[86]

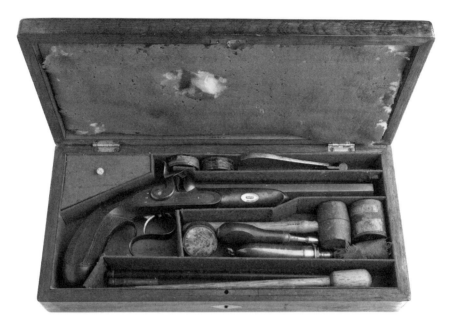

A cased smoothbore percussion pistol marked by gunsmith John Henry Happoldt of Charleston, circa 1845. *Courtesy of the Charleston Museum.*

Whatever the case, guns of the dueling style were a hot item. So hot, in fact, that one of Charleston's most prolific firearms manufacturing families, the Happoldts, began specifically marketing large-bore handguns as dueling pieces in the 1850s. They advertised the business in the *Charleston Courier* as a "maker of duelling [*sic*] pistols, derringers, percussion rifles, and shotguns." Brothers Benjamin and John Happoldt ran a lucrative firearms shop at 153 Meeting Street before moving to State Street. Eventually, John partnered with another Charleston gunsmith, J.P. Murray, operated under the name Happoldt and Murray, before ultimately taking the business to Georgia.

Indubitably, the flintlock was at the very core of duelists' traditional weaponry. A pre-carved flint stone, fixed between the jaws of the gun's cock, initiated the chain-reactive firing process. Once fired, sparks from the flint strike on the steel strike plate (or frizzen) fell into an open pan filled with powder. This ignited the pan's primer charge, which in turn sent sparks through a small hole at the breech and consequently ignited the main charge inside the barrel. Was it reliable? Well, lasting 228 years as the chief firing mechanism on all firearms, it certainly got the job done. Flintlocks, however,

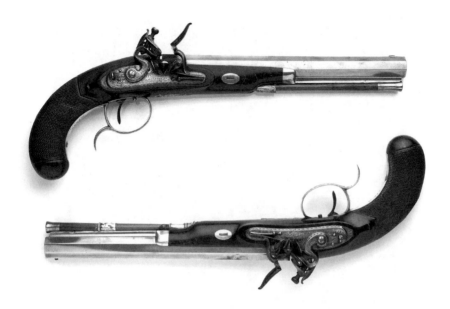

Flintlock pistols made by Georgian gunsmith Templeton Reid and belonging to John Floyd Tyler of Savannah. Though percussion caps rendered the flintlock standard obsolete, many duelists still preferred them due to an increased chance for a misfire, which counted as a shot. After serving in the War of 1812 and the subsequent American Indian wars, Tyler passed the guns over to Hugh Morris Comer with a transmittal letter stating ominously, "pistols for two, coffee for one." *Private collection, photo by Sean Money.*

were not without their flaws. On average, two shots out of every thirteen were misfires, a phenomenon usually attributed to faulty flints.[87]

Of course, under the *Code Duello*, a misfire counted as a shot no matter the cause. Rule twenty states, "In all cases a miss-fire is equivalent to a shot, and a snap or non-cock is to be considered as a miss-fire." Additionally, the flintlock's mechanics allowed for exposed gunpowder, so weather could be a considerable factor when fighting with them. Less confident duelists on occasion chose particularly humid locations in hopes of increasing their chances for an opponent's misfire. A rainy day was all the better. To be sure, the inconsistency of flintlock ignition could potentially save lives.[88]

In 1838, a revolution in priming charges came to fruition in the form of the percussion cap, a small copper casing with an even smaller filling of mercury fulminate. To activate the percussion cap, a blunt hammer replaced the flint jaws, and the cap itself fitted over a small socket known as a nipple. The impact (or percussion) on the cap from the hammer

Beginning in the 1830s, duelists rushed to modernize their pistols by converting antiquated flintlock actions to more reliable percussion cap. This cased pair marked by London gunsmith Durs Egg, circa 1800, was updated by Aiken Simmons of Charleston probably in the 1840s. *Courtesy of the Charleston Museum.*

ignited the compound inside and forced a spark through the nipple, setting off the main charge.

Since percussion caps produced a chemical ignition, they were mostly weatherproof and certainly more reliable than the older flintlock standard. Therefore, the general effects of the percussion cap on dueling were noteworthy in that the chances of a misfire dropped significantly. Governor Wilson wrote of the new percussion pistols and even hinted that this new technology was maybe a tad *too* reliable, thus granting duelists the right to refuse them. Chapter seven of his rulebook states, "The arms should be smooth-bore pistols, not exceeding nine inches in length, with flint and steel. Percussion pistols may be mutually used if agreed upon, but to object on that account is lawful." Sadly, despite Wilson's suggestion, Charleston duelists flocked to their local gunsmiths to have their pistols refurbished with fancy new percussion actions, and updated, reliable firearms soon found their way onto the dueling fields. [89]

Besides ignitions, hair triggers were at first popular addendums to duelists' pistols but fell out of favor by the early nineteenth century. A hair-trigger apparatus is a relatively simple one. Usually adjustable, the device makes the trigger itself far more sensitive to pressure. That is, a typical hair trigger would need about only one-half pound of force before discharging. In contrast, a regular trigger in a standard, large-bore pistol of the day generally required about a ten- to twelve-pound pull before going off. Surprisingly, neither the *Code Duello* nor Governor Wilson addressed the use of hair triggers, leaving the moral use of them open for debate among principals and seconds. Despite this avoidance, however, southerners roundly discouraged hair triggers. Certainly they were small and concealable, but most of all, they just *seemed* unfair.[90]

Besides the general sense of being ethically questionable, many duelists disliked the sensitivity of hair triggers, which oftentimes caused an uncontrolled or unexpected discharge. Alexander Hamilton, for example, instead of using his own pair of masterfully crafted, English-made pistols against Aaron Burr, borrowed a set from his brother-in-law, John B. Church. Why the sudden switch? Church's cased pair sported hair triggers, which Hamilton considered an asset. In the end, Hamilton really cheated only himself. Not accustomed to the trigger's feather touch, it could very well be the reason he so badly missed Burr, instead hitting a nearby tree some ten to twelve feet up.[91]

Now, whatever the improvements to a gun's firing mechanism, they were still no match for the bullet's primary delivery system—the barrel. A key component for use in nearly all duels was a pistol equipped with a smoothbore barrel, so called because of the barrel's smooth, unaltered interior. Smoothbores were vital for survival, usually insisted upon by most duelists and specifically encouraged by both the *Code Duello* and Wilson. By nature, smoothbore pistols considerably lacked the accuracy of a rifled barrel. To facilitate muzzle loading, the ball was minutely smaller than the barrel's diameter. Thus, when the pistol discharged, the lack of spiraling grooves to guide the ball caused it to tumble and bounce down the barrel, giving it an irregular, certainly unpredictable flight pattern.

Field-testing performed by the Royal Armouries in Leeds, England, reveal that large-caliber smoothbore pistols of both flintlock and percussion action do indeed strike their targets consistently, even at ranges up to twenty-five yards. However, each test recorded significant deviations in trajectory by as much as two inches or more over distances of twelve to fifteen yards. It is also vitally important to note that the RA conducted these trials in the comfortable confines of their private firing range with the pistol itself secured in a vice. A heavy, long-barreled pistol in a nervous duelist's shaky hand at the end of an unsupported, outstretched arm taking aim for his life would most certainly not produce similar results.[92]

Typically, the distance between two duelists was somewhere between ten and twenty yards, so obviously it was in a duelist's best interest to push for as large a distance apart as possible. Nevertheless, sharpshooters often regarded that anyone could get lucky. One such duelist, Lieutenant Samuel Stanton of the British Army's Ninety-seventh Regiment of Foot, wrote that if a man took his time and aimed carefully, he had a one in five chance of hitting his target even if he was a lousy shot.[93]

Of course, even though smoothbores might have been generally preferred, to say they were *always* used would be inaccurate. In the end, it was all up to the seconds to negotiate where and with what. Surprisingly, some European countries hoping to discourage dueling theorized that superiorly accurate dueling pistols would persuade potential gunfighters to think twice and actually adopted rifled pistols, considering them their national standard. In fact, matched and cased pairs of French and German antique handguns auctioned today as dueling pistols often come with rifled barrels.[94]

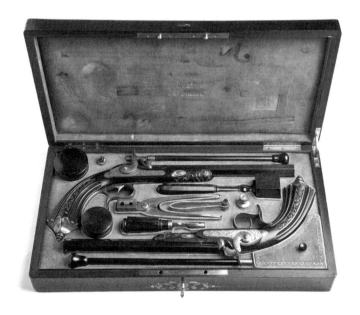

Since rifling's superior accuracy and range could almost guarantee a serious wound or fatality on the dueling field, matched pistols with rifled barrels like these made in St. Etienne, France, circa 1870, were actually adopted among many European countries as a means of deterring duels. *Courtesy of the Charleston Museum.*

Of course, no matter how high the quality, accuracy or reliability of a good dueling pistol, it was only as good as the person firing it. Unforeseen circumstances of user error and dumb luck could indeed prove helpful at times. One such duel in the early 1830s between Isaac William Hayne and Benjamin Allston (the same Benjamin Allston from the previous chapter) reflects the folly in human error. Hayne—an attorney in Charleston named for his grandfather, the Revolutionary War colonel hanged by the British in 1781—refused to disclose legal papers to Allston, a rival attorney attempting to prosecute his client. Feeling himself ignored by Hayne, Allston delivered a challenge demanding satisfaction.

After taking the field with their seconds, Allston—a bit of a braggart—insisted on loading his own pistol in an attempt to both intimidate Hayne and show off for some spectators. Unfortunately, it was a windy morning. As he flamboyantly poured his gunpowder down the barrel, Allston failed to notice a large portion of it blow away in the breeze. Hayne and Allston took their positions and fired simultaneously. Allston's bullet hit Hayne in the thigh but, thanks to its extremely weak charge, bounced off. Allston, on the other hand, was severely wounded and lived the rest of his life crippled.[95]

Today, just mentioning the word "duel" conjures up some rather stereotypical mental images of two refined blokes daintily pointing handguns at one another. But in Charleston—ostensibly more than anywhere else—there are many examples of blatantly unsophisticated, if not heterodox, forms of fighting—local cases where a mere pistol simply wouldn't do.

In 1873, editor Robert Barnwell Rhett Jr. challenged Judge William H. Cooley over a successful lawsuit he had brought against Rhett Jr.'s New Orleans newspaper, the *Picayune*. With deep family ties to Charleston, Rhett was no stranger to the ways of honor. Despite his father, Senator and "Father of Secession" Robert Barnwell Rhett Sr., being vehemently opposed to dueling, Robert's brothers, Alfred and Edmund, had already been involved in several duels in and around Charleston by this time.

In order to avoid creating a spectacle, Cooley and Rhett Jr. agreed to meet outside Louisiana borders. Both men, together with their attending seconds and surgeons, boarded a train for Bay St. Louis, Mississippi, where on July 1, Rhett and Cooley carried out their rather vicious duel. In agreement with the prearranged terms, both combatants took their places some forty yards apart on a sandy, isolated field, each armed with a double-barreled shotgun loaded with buckshot in one barrel and a large single ball in the other. Although it is unknown which barrel the two fired in the first volley, Rhett missed high and Cooley missed wide. Tragically, however, Cooley wasn't so lucky upon the second exchange. Shot through the heart, he died instantly.[96]

Perhaps just as profane, if not more so, was a duel fought in 1839 between Dr. James Decatur Pelot, of Charleston Huguenot descent, and Mr. Linver Babcock. Two days before Christmas, the two squared off on Cumberland Island, Georgia, at twenty paces distance. At the word, each aimed and fired Kentucky long rifles at each other. Dr. Pelot suffered a rather gruesome wound to the face and died the same day.[97]

Now, for many men within Charleston's upper classes, finding themselves caught up in a duel was not exactly good news—especially for those who knew themselves not to be the world's best sharpshooters. To remedy this situation, some smartly took to practicing or even hiring shooting instructors to (hopefully) increase their odds for survival. For better or worse, there were no rules or morals forbidding training. As Wilson's manual stated, any extra time or delays between challenges could indeed be "used in preparation and practice."[98]

Practicing for a duel was a justifiably wise—in some cases necessary—task for the duelist as well as his second. Clearly, if one were going to be in a gunfight for his life, he had best learn to gunfight. Around the South, practicing was customary and generally viewed as honorable. For no other reason, proper training, whether alone or with an instructor, showed a duelist's resolve and determination, further proving to his compatriots that he was willing to go the distance in order to attain satisfaction and preserve honor.

Moreover, earning a reputation as a pistol-packing crack shot was never a bad thing. For obvious reasons, marksmanship was a vital ingredient to dueling; the better a man was with his aim, the better his chances for success in the field. In fact, having good aim did as much for preventing duels as it did for fighting them. Historically, skilled sharpshooters sent far more challenges than they received, and because of their abilities, few willfully entered into a duel against them. Through sheer ability and performance, a talented gunman earned a bit more latitude when voicing his thoughts and opinions openly.

Methods for training varied from region to region, duelist to duelist. In New Orleans, for example, it was popularly rumored that medical college founder Dr. Charles Aloysius Luzenberg practiced his marksmanship by commandeering unclaimed cadavers from the local hospital, suspending them from tree limbs and then shooting at them from various distances. (This morose training method is likely the reason why Dr. Luzenberg's several challenges went unmet.) As for the locals near the Piedmont section of South Carolina near Camden, one plantation owner forged an iron silhouette of an average-height man in a dueling pose. His target of sorts eventually gave rise to the phrase "going to see the iron man," indicating someone was preparing for a duel.[99]

In Charleston, an interesting advertisement placed in the *Charleston Courier* on April 4, 1827, announced the arrival of D. Mendoza Jr. from London, an instructor of "The Art of Self Defence [*sic*] Scientifically Taught." The ad stated that "he has opened a large and commodious Room, at Mr. Gillespie's, Queen Street entrance at the private door. Mr. M will teach any Gentleman."

Curiously, nowhere does Mendoza mention exactly what is offered in his new clinic. There is certainly no suggestion of fencing, boxing, wrestling or really anything of a sporting nature. Furthermore, Mendoza capitalizes "Gentlemen," making clear his intended clientele. Thus, the nature of this advertisement may very well be a covert announcement for a new training school for duelist wannabes.

For Charleston attorney James L. Petigru, preparation was a way of life. As the state's attorney general, Petigru constantly found himself treading on unfriendly ground thanks to his outspokenness as a staunch Unionist and abolitionist sympathizer. Despite Petigru's countless opponents in the courtroom, his vigilance and resolution carried him through most controversies—at least until 1810, when Benjamin Faneuil Hunt came to town.

Emigrating from New England, Hunt studied law locally before instituting his own professional practice in 1813. In these early days, Hunt carried out his legal duties quietly, albeit diligently. However, his cordial, somewhat reserved nature turned many within the bar to believing he was a courtroom weakling. Finally, after some advice from a cousin, Hunt became a fighter, but not in a good way. In an effort to make a name for himself, he took up tormenting, even offensive litigation tactics. Eventually becoming known as "Bully Hunt," he was "bold, rude regardless of respect to opposing counsel, witnesses or clients, and unscrupulous as to the language in which he expressed his contempt; skilled in cajoling the jury and bullying the judge, a little sensitive to his own feelings and utterly without regard to the feelings of others...the lawyers of the old school were reluctant to encounter his rude assaults."[100]

Inevitably, Hunt and Petigru found themselves opposite each other on several occasions in the courtroom. Like always, Petigru's levelheadedness did not sway to Hunt's boorish methods. Even in the face of Hunt's hateful rants, Petigru outsmarted Hunt repeatedly. In fact, Petigru's keen attention and preparation eventually got the best of Hunt one fateful day in open court. In 1826, Petigru exposed several inconsistencies in Hunt's argument, leaving the Massachusetts native looking quite the fool. Not long after, Hunt sent a note to Petigru's office demanding he apologize and stating that failure to do so would result in a challenge. Petigru insisted that he would make no such apology and that his opinions of Hunt's law practice needed to be brought before the public for the sake of justice. Sure enough, Hunt called a duel with Petigru a few days later.[101]

So enraged by Hunt's challenge, Petigru took to preparing for the fight much the same way he did any court case. Petigru consulted local gunsmith John M. Happoldt, from whom he purchased a large-caliber "practice pistol" for the reported sum of $100. For the most part, the piece met all the necessary requirements for a proper duel save a smoothbore barrel. After a short while training, Petigru was somewhat of an expert, and some reports even suggest he was looking forward to his upcoming meeting with Hunt.[102]

Tragically, the ordeal between Hunt and Petigru ended horribly—but not in the expected way. Just before the fight was scheduled to occur, Petigru's

Prior to his duel with Faneuil Hunt, Charleston attorney James L. Petigru purchased this practice pistol made by local gunsmith John Michael Happoldt in 1826. *Courtesy of the Charleston Museum.*

eight-year-old son, Albert, was killed. In an emotional letter, Petigru wrote to his sister Jane:

> *My Albert,—yes Albert the child of my heart is dead…He fell from the head of the stair case down to the first floor, on Monday* [September 11, 1826] *about a quarter before 12 o'clock…The noise was heard at Mr. White's and Mrs. Gibbes'; the servants raised a cry…I looked into those eyes that had been so bright a moment before, and saw nothing but stony insensibility in them…I am crushed.*[103]

Astonishingly, Petigru's mother died just two days after little Albert's fall. Upon hearing the news of Petigru's heartbreak, Hunt immediately withdrew his challenge, and the duel never took place.

Finally, in terms of training, there were two types of duelists: those who trained for the pomp and ceremony and those who trained to kill. In revisiting the 1880 Cash-Shannon contest from chapter one, Cash's training ideals present a horrible insight into just how important he thought it was to prepare properly for a duel. The July 11 edition of the *New York Times* revealed a terrifying example of the colonel's practice regimen:

> *One of the most cold-blooded of the incidents preceding the meeting took place in the yard of Dr. Lee, who accompanied Cash as his second. For several hours before the duel, Col. Cash was practicing with his pistol to make sure of his aim on the field. For this purpose, he made use of his hopeful son, W.B. Cash, as a target. This worthy representative of Southern chivalry was placed in position, 15 paces—the distance between the principals in the duel—from his father, who fired at him with paper wads until he was able to strike the same spot six times in succession. When he left Dr. Lee's yard, after practicing on his human target, he was tolerably sure of the steadiness of his eye and his nerves.*

Chapter 7

APOLOGY ACCEPTED...OR NOT

Forgiveness in the Field of Honor

Perhaps one reason Charlestonians and many other South Carolinians seemed so eager to take the field against an adversary was their comparatively decent chances for survival. Statistically, studies of recorded duels in which shots were exchanged have shown that only about one in every five resulted in a fatality. However, of the great number of duels that did end with bullets flying, many others were absolved peacefully if not downright cordially without so much as loading a gun.[104]

One such near-duel happened in 1778 between North Carolina representative and signer of the Declaration of Independence John Penn and Henry Laurens, Charleston delegate and president of the Congress. Stunningly, the two men boarded at the same residence while in Philadelphia, even eating breakfast at the same table the morning of the duel. After the meal, the two proceeded to walk together to their fight, conversing all the while. Upon coming to a washed-out section of Fifth Street during the stroll, Penn lent a hand to the much older Laurens, helping him cross over it. As the two proceeded to Chestnut Street, they mutually realized their whole ordeal was "a foolish affair" and turned around.[105]

Definitely, occurrences such as the Laurens-Penn non-duel are isolated events. Still, even if a planned duel progressed to an actual meeting, gunplay was not always a means to an end. Frequently, in fact, not all duelists were hell-bent on complete vengeance. Sometimes just showing up for a duel was enough to satisfy an argument, since taking the field presented an honest willingness to put one's life on the line in the name of principle. Attending a duel with guns, seconds and surgeons at the ready showed a certain amount of chutzpah, and just going through all the motions of appointing seconds, exchanging letters, posting grievances, etc. was often enough to exhaust an argument. *That was the point.*

So, with all these publications describing how best to conduct one's self prior to and during a duel, was there any way to weasel out of one? Of course, there was always the easy way of bailing out by just not showing up, and despite the disastrous ramifications of such a cowardly act, that appears to be exactly what Colonel David Fanning did after challenging Andrew Hunter to a duel in 1782.

The tiff between Fanning and Hunter began several months prior amid the wilderness of the Carolina Backcountry in the waning stages of the American Revolution. Fanning, a North Carolina Loyalist described as a man whose "powers were developed under the influence of poverty, disease, and neglect without early instruction or example, and without any moral or religious training," spent his war days together with a band of fellow Tories plundering and burning civilian homesteads, even murdering a few Whigs along the way.[106]

Andrew Hunter, a Patriot well versed in the causes of American independence, was one of Fanning's biggest critics, and Fanning knew through Loyalist sources that Hunter frequently and publicly voiced derogatory remarks of him and his brutal exploits. Vowing to end his life, Fanning captured Hunter on the Pee Dee River and had his soldiers prepare a noose. While looking around for a suitable tree from which to hang their prisoner, a quick-thinking Hunter lurched free of his guard, leapt atop Fanning's prized horse and galloped away. Fanning was furious but insisted that his troops hold their fire so as not to injure his cherished "Bay Doe."[107]

Colonel Fanning brooded over the loss of his horse for the remainder of the war and, soon after the British defeat, made several futile attempts to reclaim her through legal channels. Hunter, however, was not about to give up his war prize, and the hatred between the two festered for several more weeks. Finally, a dejected Fanning challenged Hunter to a duel, the winner of which could keep the horse. Hunter immediately accepted, choosing to fight with swords on horseback at the Citadel Green.

It is curious as to why Colonel Fanning never showed for his duel with Hunter. Some texts suggest that he knew he couldn't win, while others say he refused to risk injuring the horse he had tried for so long to reclaim. Whatever the case, Fanning was never seen in Charleston again.[108]

Of course, most students of dueling etiquette would use Colonel Fanning as a prime example of what not to do. Seldom is the easiest way really the *right* way to avoid a fight. Probably the most hoped-for manner in which to terminate a progressing duel was for an opponent to fess up. Basic apologies and admissions of wrongdoing, in fact, ended plenty of quarrels long before taking up arms. Generally, appointed seconds were happy to deliver written repentances on behalf of their offenders while other times, by some miracle, the principals themselves negotiated some kind of truce while on the field. Unfortunately for the sender, any sort of apology all but guaranteed a guilty verdict in the court of popular opinion, which, for Charlestonians, was something simply impossible to endure. Additionally, apologies—whether written or not—did little in attaining the *physical* satisfaction that most duelists coveted.

The very first rule in the *Code Duello* calls upon the initial offender to express regret in order to avoid armed conflict, stating, "The first offence requires the apology." Years later, Governor Wilson hinted at this same discourse. Though never actually recommending an all-out verbal apology, he noted that thinking things through and perhaps admitting to an offense might be a wise decision. He writes in chapter two, "Gentlemen seldom insult each other, unless they labor under some misapprehension or mistake; and when you have discovered the original ground of error, follow each movement to the time of [insult], and harmony will be restored."[109]

Refreshingly, there did arise a few sporadic cases of outright refusals to duel. Of course, these instances were quite atypical inasmuch as only those with well-established, unshakeable reputations could get away with such lunacy. Senator Robert Barnwell Rhett Sr., South Carolina's "Father of Secession," consistently snubbed the various challenges presented to him, of which there were plenty given his aggressive Fire-Eater political platform. Alabama senator Jeremiah Clemens, for example, goaded Rhett feverishly in 1852, accusing him of just about everything from cowardice to flat out treason, yet Rhett calmly stood upon the Senate floor and proclaimed:

> *For twenty years I have been a member of the Church of Christ. The senator knows it—everybody knows it. I cannot and will not dishonor my religious profession. If [Clemens], or anyone else, supposes that I am so much afraid of his insults, or the opinion which requires them to be redressed in the field, as to be driven by them to abandon the profession of twenty years, he is entirely mistaken...True courage is best evinced by the firm maintenance of our principles amidst all temptations and trials.*[110]

Another lesser-known local citizen not the least bit interested in getting shot was one Captain Farrago (first name not printed). Upon being presented with a challenge to duel, Farrago took it upon himself to ensure that all of Charleston knew he would not fight. On January 8, 1792, the *City Gazette* printed Farrago's response to his challenger:

> *I have two objections to this duel matter. The one is, lest I should hurt you, and the other is, lest you should hurt me. I do not see any good it would do me to put a bullet through any part of your body. I could make no use of you when dead for any culinary purposes, as I would a rabbit or a turkey. I am no cannibal to feed upon the flesh of men. Why then shoot down a human creature of which I could make no use? A buffaloe [sic] would be better meat. For though your flesh might be delicate and tender, yet it wants that firmness and consistency which takes and retains salt. At any rate, it would not be fit for long sea voyages. You might make a good barbecue, it is true, being of the nature of a raccoon, or an opossum, but people are not in the habit of barbecuing anything human now. As for your hide, it is not worth the taking off, being little better than that of a year old colt. As to myself, I do not much like to stand in the way of anything harmful. I am under apprehension that you might hit me. That being the case, I think it most advisable to stay at a distance. If you want to try your pistols, take some object, a tree or a barn door, about my dimensions, if you hit that, send me word, and I shall acknowledge that if I had been standing in the same place, you might also have hit me.*

Now who can argue with that?

Unfortunately, dismissed or abandoned challenges among Charleston's duelists were irregular at best. In truth, most adversaries felt obligated to show their resolve and see things through to the end—or at least as close to it as possible. Surprisingly though, even after a duel was underway with pistols loaded and principals in place, there was still time enough to make peace. Sometime in the mid- to late eighteenth century, a popular forfeit-style tactic known as deloping emerged. An English corruption of a French word meaning to throw away, a deloped shot was one purposely sacrificed into either the air or ground, making an obvious statement to an opponent that no harm was intended, and fighting should therefore cease.

In short, a duelist who chose to delope allowed himself to forgo his target by deliberately firing away from his opponent, thus offering the proverbial olive branch, all the while not having to open his mouth. Initially, the *Code*

Duello grossly frowned upon deloping, as was stated in rule thirteen: "No dumb shooting or firing in the air is admissible in any case. The challenger ought not to have challenged without receiving offense; and the challenged ought, if he gave offense, to have made an apology before he came on the ground; therefore, children's play must be dishonorable on one side or the other, and is accordingly prohibited."

Thankfully, at least for duelists interested in survival, Governor Wilson's codes neither condoned nor forbade deloping. In fact, they never even mention it at all. Without a doubt, this glaring omission gave rise to the maneuver as an acceptable form of behavior, especially after 1838. Furthermore, the intentionally missed shot presented the deloping duelist as having a sort of short-term, nonviolent vulnerability, thus relaying feelings of regret. Obviously, for a foe to deliberately waste his *one* chance at satisfaction showed some element, some hint of remorse. In most circumstances, a deloped shot delivered the intended message. Other times, sadly, its point was missed entirely.

Even though many considered a duel's continuance after a deloped shot as monstrous, these forfeited discharges could unwittingly convey a starkly opposite message. That is, depending on the attitude of the enemy, deloping could be interpreted as a smug expression—that of a specific hatred or disdain for one's adversary who was not worth the cost of a bullet. Such disgust may have been a motivating factor for Ralph Isaacs of Charleston in his tragic duel with his once close comrade, Dr. Joseph Brown Ladd, in 1786.

Born in Newport, Rhode Island, in 1764, Dr. Joseph Brown Ladd was the eldest son of William Ladd, a pacifist almost to an extreme who later served as the first president of the American Peace Society in 1828. His son, Joseph, brought up in the ways of nonresistance practiced by his father, completed his studies in medicine and moved to Charleston circa 1783. Ladd seemingly fell in love with the new city but remained vigilant to the traditional ways of Charleston's elite. In a letter dated 1785, he wrote:

> *Surrounded by slaves, and accustomed to command,* [Charlestonians] *acquire a forward, dictatorial habit, which can never be laid aside. In order to judge of their dispositions, we must study them with attention. Courtesy, affability, and politeness form their distinguishing characteristics. For these, for the exercise of hospitality, and all the social virtues, I venture to assert that no country on earth has equaled Carolina.*[111]

At some point that same year, Dr. Ladd met and befriended Ralph Isaacs, of whom very little is known. What is well known, however, is that the two (for a short while anyway) were inseparable pals. As time passed, Dr. Ladd's occupation and reputation quickly accelerated him through Charleston society, and Isaacs was unable to keep up. Jealousy brewed within Isaacs, and the friction in their friendship ultimately came to a head in 1786. The general belief among historians is that sometime in late summer of that year, the two had a terrible falling out over a theater performance. Ladd's sister, Elizabeth Haskins, even wrote later that "he underwent a challenge for some frivolous cause; and, though averse to dueling from principle, yet the tyranny of public sentiment was such, that to decline the rencounter would have made him the mark of public scorn, and wholly destroyed his standing and influence in society."[112]

As the argument progressed, Isaacs set out to damage the good doctor's name. Fed up by October, Dr. Ladd angrily took the argument public in the October 14, 1786 edition of the *Charleston Morning Post and Daily Advertiser*, publishing a hate-filled letter directly addressing Isaacs. Calling him, among other things, a "despicable viper," "ungrateful villain" and "rash boy," Ladd, in an utter rejection of his father's former teachings of peace, continued:

> *I account it as one of the greatest misfortunes of my life that I ever became intimate with such a man, and as I move in a sphere of life and character far superior to you, I from this time, not only renounce the whole circle of your acquaintance, but disdain to speak to any man who hereafter takes you by the hand. I leave you to your own reflections. I leave you to your insignificance.*

Naturally, Isaacs responded two days later via the same paper:

> *[His] publication, the pure result of a maddened brain…The self-created Doctor impeaches me with having injured his character—brands me with the sin of ingratitude—is lavish in conferring on me the most opprobrious appellations, and finally boasts of the essential services I received at his hands. I confidently assert that Dr. Ladd is a dangerous imposter—that he is at this moment under pecuniary obligations to me, and should consequently be considered as an object of detestation and abhorrence. I dare boldly affirm that the advent of a little time will convince the world, that the self-created Doctor is as blasted a scoundrel as ever disgraced in humanity.*

Accepting the inevitable challenge, the two faced off with pistols at an undisclosed location some weeks later. However, clearly not possessing the same anger he had exhibited for the local paper, a somewhat forlorn Ladd deloped his shot, unwilling to kill his one-time best friend. Whether or not Dr. Ladd actually meant the sacrifice as a purely apologetic gesture will forever remain unknown, but even if it were, its solemnity was completely lost on Isaacs.

Likely viewing his enemy's delopement as a sneering shrug of supremacy over his own commonality, Isaacs became enraged at Ladd's supposed audacity. Caring not for this grandiose show, Isaacs took aim and blasted away, his bullet shattering Dr. Ladd's kneecap. Sadly, Ladd's severe leg wound became gangrenous during his recognizance, and he soon after died at his residence on Church Street.[113]

The Ladd-Isaacs duel is merely one example of a well-meaning gesture gone awry. Therefore, this event brings to light a serious question: what was there to do when an apology would not do under any circumstances? The *Duello* never directly addresses this dilemma, and Governor Wilson wrote only a few words on the matter, noting, "The Challengee has no option when negotiation has ceased, but to accept the Challenge."[114]

In a 1998 production for the History Channel, author Grahame Long (in costume) portrayed Ralph Isaacs during his 1786 duel with Dr. Joseph Brown Ladd. *Photo by Laurens Smith.*

Whatever an individual's thoughts, the duel between George McDuffie and William Cumming is perhaps one of the greatest examples of unaccepted apologies known in South Carolina. Described as "taciturn" and "disposed to lecture" even in conventional conversation, McDuffie earned a law degree in 1814, in 1818 served the state Congress and eventually became a United States senator and governor of South Carolina by 1834.[115]

During McDuffie's days in the United States House, however, his political path crossed that of Colonel William Cumming, a Georgia planter, War of 1812 veteran and a man once described by John C. Calhoun as "subject to hereditary insanity from his mother." What erupted from a heated and well-publicized political debate over nullification in 1821 soon boiled over into not one but *three* separate duels between McDuffie and Cumming, two of which ended in gunfire.[116]

The first meeting between the two took place in June 1822. At first fire, McDuffie appeared to delope his shot into the ground, sending a cloud of dust into the air near the halfway point between himself and Cumming. Believing his action sufficient to end the duel, McDuffie turned slightly away from his opponent. Alas, without the least bit of hesitation or consideration for McDuffie's delopement, Cumming shot McDuffie, lodging a bullet in his back.[117]

Fortunately for McDuffie, he (mostly) recovered from the near fatal shot, but from that point on there was no more Mr. Nice Guy. McDuffie stubbornly proceeded to post Cumming relentlessly both with placards and in the newspapers. Even John Quincy Adams wrote in his memoirs, "This feud has become a sort of historical incident…The seconds, surgeons, and others have got involved in the dispute, and all have become the laughing-stock of the public throughout the Union, except in South Carolina and Georgia, where the parties are feasted and toasted 'alive or dead.'"[118]

Notwithstanding, McDuffie pushed on until Cumming sent a second challenge—this one intent on putting McDuffie squarely in his grave. A lengthy arbitration of terms between the seconds ensued. Finally, upon taking the field, McDuffie's second called Cumming's shooting stance into question, as he tended to take on a semi-crouched position, effectively making him a smaller target. Unable to agree, the parties cancelled the contest but not before swearing to meet again.[119]

Sure enough, McDuffie and Cumming met for a third and last time later that autumn. Cumming this time was required to alter his stance to a proper and upright profile. It didn't help. At the word "Fire," McDuffie missed Cumming completely but had his own left arm shattered by Cumming's shot. At long last, the two mercifully declared reciprocal satisfaction and went home.[120]

Shockingly, the series of contests with Colonel Cumming was not enough to put an end to McDuffie's dueling penchant. Some years later, he proceeded to challenge Congressman Thomas Metcalfe of Kentucky. Allowed his choice of weapons, Metcalfe chose long rifles at a distance of thirty yards. McDuffie's second, Mr. James Hamilton Jr., ultimately refused on the grounds that his principal's weakened arm—a result of the wound suffered in the first duel with Cumming—made it difficult for him to properly hold and fire a rifle. The duel never happened.[121]

Hopefully, of course, unlike the McDuffie-Cumming affair, once a duel occurred (and assuming both combatants survived it), there was to be no more fuss. Charleston gentlemen adhering to their duelist heritage had an uncanny knack for reconciliation, and amazingly, those involved typically considered the matter permanently settled at this point, apology or not. As if by some rite of magic, a concluded duel assured everyone that grievances were rested, honor was restored and final satisfaction was attained absolutely. Moreover, the rules within both the *Code Duello* and Wilson's manual emphatically concurred that a duel contented the antagonisms of the duelists and the conflict between them was no longer alive. Likewise, duelists were expected to remain cordial to each other after a duel, each granting the same respects to the other as they would toward any other one of their friends or colleagues. To its credit, a duel did well in smoothing over quarrels, and there are many instances of one-time dueling enemies actually becoming cordial comrades after settling their score on the field.

As children, Olin M. Dantzler and Laurence Keitt spent their boyhoods playing together and, after a brief time apart for college, found their way back to South Carolina and into a life of politics. In this arena, however, the two often differed in opinions and, unfortunately, soon became rivals. Thus, it serves as really no surprise that the lifelong friends, each steeped in southern tradition, would eventually fight a duel, nearly killing each other as a result. Still, theirs is indeed a rather astonishing (and maybe extreme) example of personal consideration. For them, the duel was strict political business, and not once did either man allow their fight to influence their compassion for each other. Immediately after their duel, in fact, the two seamlessly reverted to their original working relationship and jointly took up the cause for the Confederate States after secession in 1860.[122]

Remarkably, Dantzler and Keitt remained close as regimental officers each within the Twentieth South Carolina Volunteer Infantry. Together, they served valiantly at areas around Charleston, including Morris Island and James Island. Tragically, after traveling to Virginia in 1864 to assist in the defense of Richmond, both Dantzler and Keitt fell mortally wounded within forty-eight hours of each other (Keitt at Cold Harbor and Dantzler at the Bermuda Hundred campaign). Their bodies were soon after collected, crated and sent home aboard the same train. Poignantly, the remains of Colonels Keitt and Dantzler were laid practically side by side in Tabernacle Cemetery near Saint Stephens, where they rested for several years until Keitt's remains were exhumed and relocated to nearby West End Cemetery.[123]

Chapter 8

Sadism and the South

The Malevolent Mêlées of Men...and Women

Even though dueling was a universal occurrence by the 1750s and continued relatively unabated well throughout the next 130 years, there were plenty of differing regional attitudes toward it. In the North, hard laws and even harder enforcement of them ushered the act of dueling into a comparatively early extinction. Take, for example, the extremely tough laws passed under the Act of Massachusetts in 1729 that sentenced anyone found guilty of conspiring to a duel to be "carried in a cart to the gallows with a rope about the neck." Once there, the offender sat under guard for no less than one hour still with the noose tight around his throat. As if that wasn't enough, the harsh law was updated in 1784 to include: "That when it shall appear by the coroner's inquest that any person hath been killed in fighting a duel...the body of such person so killed [is to] be immediately secured and buried without a coffin, with [a] stake drove through the body, at or near the usual place of execution, or shall deliver the body to any surgeon or surgeons, to be dissected."[124]

After July 11, 1804, the shock of Alexander Hamilton's death at the hands of Aaron Burr spread rapidly throughout New Jersey, New York and on up through the New England states, and the folly of dueling there eventually garnered too much negative attention to make it a viable recourse in northern society. Duels fought farther south in the middle Atlantic and Chesapeake regions certainly occurred more often than in their neighboring northern states, yet these contests seemed to gravitate mostly toward affairs of political discourse.[125]

For would-be duelists in the South, however, it was open season. Beginning sometime around the late colonial period, most of the established European rules for dueling had been lost in translation among the Lowcountry gentry. After all, from a Charlestonian's perspective, who could say who was honorable or who was not? Most local duelists worked for a living, which, by classical definition, made them non-gentlemen to begin with. Around the state, lawyers fought lawyers over court rulings, newspaper editors dueled over whose story was more accurate and even middle-class citizens dueled to make themselves look like upper-class citizens.

Dueling at South Carolina College (now University of South Carolina) was especially concerning. By 1825, in fact, Headmaster Thomas Cooper had instilled mandatory suspensions on any student sending or accepting dueling challenges and outright expelled several students for going as far as appointing seconds. Alas, his efforts were only moderately successful in saving students' lives—two of which were ended by duels in 1834.[126]

On the whole, there never seemed to be a shortage of hotheaded pistoleers in Charleston, each perfectly willing to push the envelope of appropriate dueling etiquette despite good manners and privacy. Debatably, of course, all this wanton carnage might have been thanks in part to duelists' widespread acceptance of guns. Pistols, to be sure, were easy to use, and their employment in formal dueling beginning in the eighteenth century threw open the doors to just about anyone.

Making matters so much worse was that with the relative ease and public acceptance of dueling, there slowly emerged a half-baked addiction to it. Charleston elites could twist just about anything into a personal grievance and did so often and on purpose just to get another onto the field. The wealthy planter class, for example, loathed thriftiness and hated misers even more. Therefore, to so much as hint at anything financially frugal toward these Lowcountry barons quickly invited a challenge.

Upper-echelon politicos fared far worse, often construing disagreements with their particular platforms as personal attacks. These, it appeared, were the habitual duelists—professionals as it were—who had many southerners on watch. Andrew Jackson, whose fiery Irish Presbyterian mother instilled in him at a young age the critical value of defending one's character to the death, carried a penchant for dueling unmatched by most other high-profile American politicians. Alexander K. McClung, nephew of Chief Justice John Marshall and short-term appointee to Zachary Taylor's administration, killed untold dozens of opponents (several from the same family) before committing suicide with his own dueling pistol in 1855.[127]

The Duel, ink drawing by Edward Windsor Kemble, 1887. Proper dueling etiquette began to wane in the years following the Civil War. Impromptu duels often forewent traditional protocol, including weaponry. Here, two duelists, both without seconds, are adorned in loose overcoats and hats to obscure their profile, and each is armed with a multi-shot revolver. *Courtesy of Library of Congress.*

When it comes to discussing local aficionados, however, perhaps James Hamilton Jr. is Charleston's best offering. It is not known just how many duels Hamilton fought exactly. Many sources credit him with fighting in at least fourteen, while others cite only one. Whatever the actual count, one thing is certain: as a lawyer, a soldier, a politician, a nullifier and a Charlestonian, trouble seemed to find him wherever he went.[128]

As Carolina folklore suggests, Hamilton dueled in a way no other man really could—meaning he was actually *good* at it. Possessing a flawless track record so to speak, it is said that Hamilton managed to wound nearly every one of his opponents without killing any of them while he himself emerged without so much as a scratch. What's more, his field expertise was known everywhere among the dueling class, and Hamilton was glad to offer his duelist proficiency to those who asked, once traveling as far as New Jersey to assist a friend as the appointed second.[129]

Born in 1786 the privileged son of a Charleston planter father and a hereditarily wealthy mother, Hamilton's salad days did not last long. By the time he was a mere teenager, Hamilton's mother, Elizabeth, was dead and his father, a former Continental army major who had crossed the Delaware River with Washington in 1776, was losing financial control of his plantation. Moreover, a lengthy chain of tropical storms and hurricanes in the late 1790s consistently flooded the property, ruined its crops and consequently forced young James to take on considerable management responsibilities in the wake of his father's depression.[130]

About this same time, "Jimmy" got his first taste of dueling, albeit at his father's expense. While entertaining guests at his home, a liquor-saturated argument between the old major and John Bowman, a distant relative, gave way to a haphazard duel that occurred right on the front yard in full view of Jimmy and the entire house staff. Completely forgoing the usual procedures, the pair drunkenly blasted away until Major Hamilton fell, severely wounded. His right shin shattered, surgeons soon after amputated the major's mangled leg, sending him even further into emotional turmoil.[131]

By 1811, the Hamilton plantation had been broken up and sold off. Seemingly unaffected by his family failures, however, Jimmy, now in his early twenties, moved rather seamlessly into the life of a city gentleman. Putting his failed planter upbringing behind him, Hamilton excelled both socially and professionally. In Charleston, he studied law, and his new vocation as a local attorney soon helped launch a prolific political career, serving first as mayor before moving up to the state legislature and then on to the U.S. Congress in 1822. By 1830, Hamilton, with his "striking good looks" and "natural charm," returned to South Carolina as its governor.[132]

During this entire rise to power, however, Hamilton never seemed to give up his father's fighting ways. As he was a practicing lawyer by 1812, the second outbreak of hostilities between Britain and the United States called to his inner soldier. Hamilton traveled north to New York, earning a commission as a lieutenant under General George Izard. While in service of the army, Hamilton married Charleston's own Elizabeth Mathews Heyward, granddaughter of Thomas Heyward Jr. and partial heir to one of the largest rice fortunes in the Lowcountry.

It was during this engagement that Hamilton fought and won his first duel against a New York dilettante named William Gracie. Acting on a rumor, Hamilton accused Gracie of inappropriately wooing his fiancée and subsequently challenged him to take the field. Elizabeth herself tried her best to intervene by swearing to Gracie's naiveté, but not even that stopped Hamilton from shooting him. Struck in the leg, Gracie carried a limp rest of his life.[133]

Decades later, the overwhelming stress of the Nullification Crisis turned Hamilton from debonair to demonic. More and more Hamilton seemed to lose his grasp on courtesy and reason. Once an ardent Jacksonian, the Tariffs of 1828 and 1832 embittered Hamilton against the president and soured him to the point of extreme anti-federalism. His speeches by this time were not so much orations as they were flat-out verbal offensives, often lashing out brutally against anyone—elected or not—who was crazy enough to oppose his anti-tariff convictions. Obviously, his anger made him a menace to those on the receiving end of his rants, and naturally, the challenges flew. By the time South Carolina repealed its Nullification Ordinance in 1833, untold dozens of dueling opportunities had come Hamilton's way, but hard evidence of just how many fights actually materialized is disappointingly fleeting.

However, it is entirely likely by this time that Hamilton had taken the field of honor more than once. In fact, a good number of Hamilton's dueling challenges were turned down, thus indicating his adversaries knew him as a skilled and willing duelist. For example, after sitting through yet another one of Hamilton's particularly angry, two-hour-plus spiels before Congress, political rival Henry Martindale openly ridiculed him and his ideas of states' rights. After the rebuttal, Hamilton challenged Martindale on the spot, but the New Yorker quickly refused, citing his strong religious beliefs. This decline was, of course, a lame cop-out. Martindale was no more devout than Hamilton was, but probably well aware of Hamilton's dueling prowess, Martindale keenly chose to invent an excuse rather than face the business end of Hamilton's pistol.[134]

Occasionally, men similar to Hamilton's father who found themselves embedded in terrifically heated exchanges allowed their rage to take control, systematically mooting dueling etiquette and social graces. What happened on the night of August 16, 1771, is one such instance of protocol gone pear-shaped. While spending their evening at a place described only as "a genteel house of entertainment in St. Michael's Alley," two local physicians, Drs. John Haley and Peter Delancey, found themselves at odds. Haley, an Irishman loyal to the American cause for independence, had spent the better part of the night rebuking Delancey, a British Loyalist. Finally, enough was enough, and Delancey loudly insulted Haley's character "by giving him the 'lie.'"[135]

In a fit of rage, Haley instantly abandoned all the polite formalities of a duelist, and his immediate challenge offered no customary courtesies like appointed seconds, surgeons, a proper venue or even a period of negotiation. Instead, Haley "proposed that they should go together to an upper room, alone," and "fight with pistols." The two adjourned. Moments later, two near-simultaneous shots boomed throughout the house and into the adjacent alley. After a few tense moments, Haley emerged from the room, leaving Delancey's body sprawled across a table, dead from a single shot to the chest.[136]

Interestingly, a sword fight broke out thirty years later between two French Huguenots again on St. Michael's Alley, just a few yards from the house where Dr. Haley died. A theater manager listed as "Placide" and a Mr. Douvilliers (first name not printed), an operatic actor, took to the street in what one witness described as "a perfect picture of a picturesque combat." Many happenstance spectators thought that perhaps the two were rehearsing for a performance—until real blood started spilling. Despite their reportedly considerable wounds and their bodies having to be carried from the alley, the two ultimately survived.[137]

Sadly, duels of an anarchic nature were not altogether unusual, isolated events among the gentlemanly citizens of the Lowcountry. In fact, the two aforementioned conflicts are merely a pair of examples of how Charlestonians viewed dueling as an exercise wide open to interpretation. For the purists, there was the pomp and ceremony. For the others, though, fast action and hot powder were more important than proper procedure.

John Laurens of Charleston, son of Henry Laurens of Continental Congress fame, found himself in a rather serious confrontation with General Charles Lee in the summer of 1778. After Lee's inexplicable retreat at the Battle of Monmouth and near complete failure to follow Washington's orders, he was court-martialed, convicted and temporarily furloughed from service. Humiliated, Lee carried his case to Congress in hopes that it would overturn his guilty verdict, but his attempts fell short. Slighted and angry, Lee carelessly resorted to publicly lambasting General Washington's leadership skills to anyone who would listen.[138]

St. Michael's Alley, just south of Broad Street, Charleston. The extremely narrow western end of the alley at Meeting Street is barely wide enough for a single car. Due to its seclusion and obscurity, its popularity as a dueling lane remains a widespread myth. *Courtesy of Library of Congress.*

John Laurens, a close colleague of Washington, having served as his aide-de-camp after the Battle of Brandywine, took special exception to Lee's criticisms. For him at least, the general's insults were unforgivable. Laurens was so infuriated, in fact, that at one point he went so far as to suggest hand-to-hand judicial combat in front of a court, but thankfully, a friend talked him out of it. Bowing to the wishes of his peers, Laurens decided to handle the situation as only proper gentlemen should. He sent a note on December 3 challenging Lee to duel, allowing three weeks to pass before fighting it out.[139]

On January 26, 1779, the *South Carolina Gazette* published a short announcement stating, "A duel was lately fought in Philadelphia between Major General Lee and Colonel John Laurens, son to the late president of Congress, in which the former was dangerously wounded; the Colonel received only a slight wound in the arm."

The newspaper unfortunately left out all the gritty details of the duel. Clearly though, Laurens saw Lee's behavior toward General Washington as monstrous and thus believed it necessary to push the bounds of tradition, all in the name of satisfaction. When the pair ultimately met on December 23, Lee, Laurens and their seconds reviewed the duel's terms. With one pistol each, Lee and Laurens would walk toward each other (each on a collision course with his opponent's muzzle) and fire at a time and distance of his own choosing. At the word, the two began walking, eventually closing to within five paces of each other before firing.

Although seriously hurt, Lee insisted that satisfaction was not at hand and the duel should continue. Laurens consented despite his own injury, but the seconds angrily objected and mercifully intervened. After a conference (while both Laurens and Lee sat bleeding), the parties thankfully decided the duel was over.[140]

Some years later in 1852, Robert Leckie and a Mr. Hall (first name not printed) got into a fierce argument—one that included more than its fair share of insults and foul language. While the object of the quarrel is unknown, the fallout was obviously too much for Leckie's patience. The next morning, as reported by the *Charleston Mercury*, Leckie borrowed a six-barreled revolver (known as a pepperbox), employed a local gunsmith to inspect and load the piece and then, under the accompaniment of a partner, "proceeded to Mr. Hall's place of business in King Street, called him to the door, and demanded satisfaction. Mr. Hall expressed his willingness to give him all the satisfaction he desired, but reminded him that this was no proper place for the settlement."

Pepperbox pistols (so called because of their large, revolving cylinders resembling pepper mills) could fire several shots by utilizing multiple barrels, each housed within manually rotated cylinders. *Courtesy of the Charleston Museum.*

As the pair made their way down King Street turning left on Beaufain, they stopped, paced off no more than six feet distance, drew their guns and fired multiple shots at each other:

> *At Mr. Hall's second shot, Mr. Leckie, placing his hand to his right side, retreated into the store of Mr. S.W. DeLand...After a brief pause, Mr. Hall passed by the door, on his way return to King Street, which Mr. Leckie observing, stepped out, fired a third shot at his antagonist's back, and then retreated within the door.*

In defense, Hall returned fire and missed, but it didn't matter. As it was, Hall's second shot—fired during the initial exchange—had already pierced Leckie's liver. Bleeding profusely out the side of his abdomen, Leckie eventually collapsed on the sidewalk and died within a half hour.[141]

Never minding insults to character or morality, it is sad that sometimes even the most asinine arguments found their way to the dueling grounds. In 1870, for example, Ludlow Cohen, a merchant in his early thirties, and Richard Aiken, a sixty-plus-year-old Lowcountry planter, fought an unusually angry duel at Brampton Plantation outside Savannah. The seconds did not even attempt to settle the issue before the shooting started, as their principals had previously assured both there would be no talk of forgiveness. So troubling was Cohen and Aiken's resolution to fight that the *New York Times* picked up the story on August 28:

> *Four Shots were fired after each of which propositions were made and questions asked as to whether the parties were satisfied, to which the answer was given, "No." At the fifth shot, Mr. Cohen fired immediately at the word, his antagonist receiving a wound in the right side, which passed through the abdomen, cutting the intestines. Mr. Cohen gradually dropped his pistol arm to his side and sank upon the ground.*

So, what was Aiken and Cohen's argument over? Cohen lost his life over the innocuous results of a sailboat race. It was the last fatal duel fought in Georgia.[142]

Another tragic (albeit now rather famous) duel involved South Carolina College student James G. Adams, killed by his best friend, Govan Roach, over scraps of food in the school dining hall:

> *They were very intimate friends; they sat opposite each other in the Steward's hall at the table. When the bell rang and the door was opened, the students rushed in, and it was considered a matter of honor, when a man got hold of a dish of butter or bread, or any other dish, it was his. Unfortunately, Roach and Adams sat opposite each other, and both caught hold of a dish of trout at the same moment. Adams did not let go; Roach held onto the dish. Presently Roach let go of the dish and glared fiercely at Adams face, and said, "Sir, I will see you after supper."*[143]

After the meal, the pair exchanged harsh words, at which point Adams was overheard saying, "This is enough, sir, and you will hear from me."

When the two eventually met at Lightwood Knot Springs just outside Columbia, each took their places and, at the word, fired simultaneously, with each receiving wounds in the hip. Adams died. Roach, though victorious, remained hobbled for life.[144]

Now, with all this talk of dueling men, is it safe to assume that women had no place on the field of honor? Since ancient history, women have never been strangers to combat: Judge Deborah, "Black Agnes" Randolph, Joan of Arc, Anne Bonny and the list goes on. Dueling among women—though sporadic—took place in Europe as well as America. However, European males often viewed female duels as typically more folly than fight—sometimes a mere spectacle carried out for amusement. Be that as it may, it certainly did not stop the Countess of Polignac and Lady de Nesle from shooting it out in the Versailles garden in 1721; the rather bloody knife fight between Mademoiselles d'Aiguillon and de Guignes in 1772; or Madame Moussin, who reportedly killed (at least) three male opponents in separate duels outside Paris. Even before this modern viewpoint, women were occasionally granted a venue for judicial combat. Here, however, the rules were altered a bit. If the female combatant were faced with a male opponent, for example, he had to fight within the confines of a small-diameter, waist-deep pit.[145]

American women—primarily southern ones—were no less vicious and took matters just as seriously as their men did. For history's sake though, female duelists had an unfortunate knack for avoiding publicity, especially in the traditionally male-driven societies of the eighteenth and nineteenth centuries. It was men, after all, who were responsible for a woman's honor, and it was up to them to preserve it and fight for it when necessary.

Furthermore, men controlled the newspapers, most of which viewed women dueling as nothing more than spoiled-sport hissy fits. Occasionally, editors ran reports of duels between women from far-off places like Mexico or Paris, but these were usually intended as stories of curiosity only. Not to say that women never fought it out on deadly ground though. On April 4, 1882, the Sumter newspaper the *Watchman and Southron* reported:

A deadly duel between two women, to decide which of the twain should have solely the affection of a man who had been paying attention to them both. Last night they met, and, after a desperate hand-to-hand conflict, one was left dead upon the field, although as the sequel proved, her defeat was encompassed by means of foul play: Robert S. Elby, a young farmer in humble life, lived near the scene of the tragedy. A year ago he was an

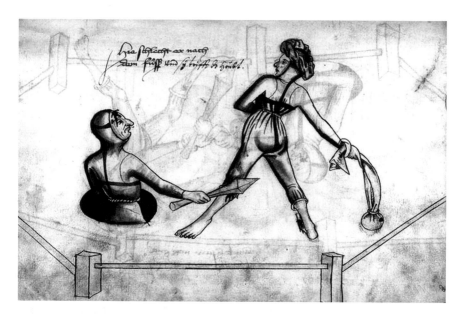

Judicial combat allowed for the occasional female participant. However, in an effort to even the field, male opponents were sometimes ordered to fight while confined to a shallow pit, as shown in this 1459 illustration by Hans Talhoffer. *Courtesy of Wikimedia Commons/public domain.*

ardent suitor for the hand of Miss Gracie Mills, who lived just over the South Carolina line; but although he courted her frequently, she would not marry him.

Worse than that, the *Edgefield Advertiser* detailed an incredibly brutal duel between Mrs. Julia Tripp and her sister-in-law, Mrs. Jacob Silvers, as late as 1909. The women, each armed with a revolver in one hand and a knife in the other, shot and slashed away at each other over Silvers's estranged husband. Both women died. The article concludes: "There were ten bullet wounds and one cut on the body of Mrs. Tripp. Mrs. Silvers had a bullet wound in the chest and several knife slashes…Eight empty shells and two cartridges were found indicating that [one] revolver was emptied and reloaded."

Chapter 9

CIVICS AND SERMONS

Dueling's Naysayers and Ne'er-Do-Wells

Even in the Middle Ages, there were plenty of government measures and other group movements aimed at curbing trial by combat, wagers of battle and most other forms of dueling activity. Sir Francis Bacon, attorney general to James I, stated publicly even as early as 1615:

> *The first motive is a false and erroneous imagination of honour and credit therefore the King in his last proclamation doth most aptly and excellently call them bewitching Duels. For if we can judge of it truly, it is no better than a sorcery that enchanteth the spirits of young men, that bear great minds with a false show, "species falsa"; and a kind of satanical illusion and apparition of honour against religion, against law, against moral virtue.*[146]

While arguments such as Bacon's received only casual attention, if any at all, most faith-based groups needed look no further than the sixth commandment for a solid reason to condemn this form of controlled killing. Other Christian organizations and congregations unsurprisingly reviled the practice on grounds of willful murder or, moreover, suicide. A fiery 1823 sermon by Reverend Samuel Gilman, for example, delivered at the Second Independent Church in Charleston suggested that duelists were all but abandoning their faith:

> *Oh Christianity! divine but neglected Christianity!…When wilt thou cause every man to be regarded as the brother and the friend of every man? When*

wilt thou come and speak repose to the tumult of human passions?…
When wilt thou enforce the conviction that highminded honour, and manly
fortitude, and genuine courage, are perfectly compatible with the bloodless
triumphs of the Gospel, and that everything gallant, public-spirited, and
godlike in the human character, would not necessarily be abolished from the
world…We will weep for the World.[147]

Earlier in 1821, the Reverend Mason Locke Weems, a Pennsylvania book peddler and author ordained in the Protestant Episcopal Church, published a scathing pamphlet entitled *God's Revenge Against Dueling, or The duelists* [sic] *looking glass: Exhibiting that gentlemanly mode of turning the corner, in features altogether novel and admirably calculated to entertain and instruct the American youth*. The work—complete with illustrations—was intended as a direct address to young men, asking them to abandon their "goatish lust" and "satanic pride."[148]

To Weems's credit, he appears to be one of the first scholars to tie dueling together with suicide, writing, "If they can not muster patience, to wait long enough to kill themselves with whiskey and tobacco they will give way to their brutish passions and provoke some other madman to blow out their brains." Sadly, his efforts were of little relevance in Charleston, and most southern readers agreed that Weems's diatribes were good for a laugh and little else. Certainly not helping his credibility issues were most of his previous anecdotal writings, which were either suspicious confabulations or outright inventions (his most famous perhaps being the tale of young George Washington axing the cherry tree, of which he wrote circa 1800). He died in Beaufort, South Carolina, a bit of a laughingstock.[149]

Extensive as dueling was by the turn of the nineteenth century, soft grumblings from those against it slowly solidified into more concerted, serious arguments. In Charleston, both the Revolutionary Society and the South Carolina Society of the Cincinnati appointed a joint committee in 1803 with the common goal of petitioning legislature to make at least *some* effort to restrain dueling. The group drafted a petition and collected more than four thousand signatures before presenting its case to its elected representatives. Furthermore, the committee was successful in circulating letters to local clergy persuading them to preach against all manner of violence—dueling especially. Despite their best efforts though, both societies failed to convince the state government of their convictions, and no real laws against dueling were considered.[150]

Down but not out, the Society of the Cincinnati committee tried again in 1804 to curb the dueling contagion. This time, however, it abandoned its

Arrah now, my honey! and that Shot you! appeared in Mason Locke Weems's pamphlet, *God's Revenge Against Dueling* in 1820 as a humorous approach to condemning dueling as both murder and suicide. *Private collection, photo by Sean Money.*

original idea of criminalizing duelists when a fatality occurred and instead took a financial approach in its suggested punishments. The new bill for the most part ignored the "life of the survivor," meaning the duelist as a person was not to be prosecuted. His property, on the other hand, was to be forfeited immediately "to the obligation providing for the family of his deceased antagonist."[151]

Charles Cotesworth Pinckney, a former delegate to the Constitutional Convention, presented this bill before the state government—and failed miserably. As reported in the *Charleston Courier* later that year:

> *No law has yet been passed relative to duels; and the practice of killing men in single combat and of acquitting the survivors continues. South Carolina loses four or five of its citizens almost every year and sometimes embryo citizens; for lads have fought duels, who were too young to give their votes at elections or to make their wills. They dispose of their lives when they are not legally competent to dispose of their property.*

Between 1798 and 1804, the state's general assembly received over twenty-one anti-dueling petitions from all areas of the state, including several from Charleston. None succeeded. Even though Aaron Burr's killing of Alexander Hamilton tweaked the nation's attention toward dueling's maliciousness, Charlestonians remained more or less unaffected, and their apathy evoked fervor among local clergymen, whose condemnation of dueling, its participants and its bystanders boiled over from the pulpits on a regular basis.

On October 28, 1804, for example, Reverend Thomas Frost of St. Philip's Church delivered a noteworthy sermon in which he used a passage from the book of 1st Samuel: "I have transgressed the commandment of the Lord, and thy words: because I feared the people, and obeyed their voice." Of course, by choosing this particular verse, Frost did his best to not only blame the duelist for murder but also place equal accountability onto the general public for their part in continually enabling the tradition.[152]

Later that September, Charlestonians were presented with *The Memorial Against Dueling*, a pamphlet signed by seventeen various "prominent citizens" and addressed to "The Honorable, The President, and the other members of the senate of the State of South Carolina." In its rambling conclusion (after numerous paragraphs condemning both dueling and duelists alike), the letter makes its request:

> *Therefore we pray...that you would in your wisdom, provide such remedies, as may, effectually, destroy the evil practice...by regulations wisely calculated to protect the fame and feelings of the innocent and injured person; and to punish, rigorously the bold offender, who shall dare to lift his hand against his neighbor, and shed his blood, in a duel, in violation of Divine law, and the law of his country.*[153]

Unsurprisingly, rituals of and reasons for dueling were still deeply delicate matters among Charleston's gentry; bureaucratic involvement was not welcome in such private, personal affairs. Furthermore, most locals agreed that without any real and provable protections for character, dueling must continue. Thus, efforts to quell dueling in South Carolina floundered repeatedly even in the fallout of Hamilton-Burr. In fact, it was another long and deadly eight years before the state at last acted, albeit casually, upon the various cries of its electorate.

In 1812, a bill prohibiting dueling in all forms passed into law. As it stated, anyone convicted of participating in a duel was to be fined $2,000 and face imprisonment for twelve months. Additionally, both guilty parties were banned from holding "any office of honor, profit, or trust" and were furthermore prohibited from practicing law, medicine or divinity.[154]

Of course, no matter how stern the written language, this early mandate was ceremonial at best, useless at worst. After all, the 1812 state legislation against dueling was only enforceable on those convicted of it—a caveat that would prove near impossible to meet in nineteenth-century Charleston. Making matters even more difficult was the fact that, in truth, laws against dueling were roundly ignored on a global scale and had been for centuries. Louis XIV, for instance, tried at least three separate times to quell dueling among his subjects from 1643 to 1670, but his ordinances went mostly unobserved. Queen Anne also voiced her opposition to dueling in 1718, but the House of Lords bluntly rejected her efforts. Why should Charleston be any different?[155]

Notwithstanding, a group of Charlestonians in the 1820s formed the Standing Committee of the Anti-Dueling Society, holding regular meetings in the federal courthouse. The mission was simple: to succeed where so many other groups had failed and to put a definitive end to dueling. Endeavoring to bring about new laws to replace the older, unenforced ones, the society took to the newspapers, persistently blaming their role in keeping the duelists' traditions alive. One example printed in the *Charleston Courier* on July 30, 1827, noted, "Such publications rank high among the causes which keep up the practice of Duelling [*sic*]. And Whereas, the right to insert such publications has no more to do with the liberty of the press, than the right to violate the security or happiness of individuals in any other mode, has with the enjoyment of civil liberty."

Unfortunately, the society's members failed to notice the irony of using the city's newspapers in order to criticize them, and editors soon began rejecting their requests for print space.

Anti-duelists suffered yet another major setback, this time in 1849 upon the death of Governor John Lyde Wilson. His passing only re-evoked Charleston's high regard for dueling. Adding to his legacy, several printing firms commemoratively republished Wilson's *Code of Honor* in 1858, thus reigniting Charleston's duelist culture, whose taste for violence would continue into the tumultuous 1860s.

Alas, just like the American Patriots during the Revolution, dueling among Confederate soldiers and officers was not altogether rare. Edwin Calhoun of Company C, Sixth South Carolina Cavalry, recalled in a memoir that while encamped at Cub Run outside Washington in the winter of 1861, "Nothing of interest occurred at this camp…Major Seibles and Captain Bland fought a duel. Seibles was wounded in the breast but soon recovered."[156]

It is unclear just how many duels occurred within the Confederate military during the war. If judging solely by this one soldier's writings, one could easily assume they were just a normal part of everyday life. Whatever its frequency, dueling was most certainly prevalent among the Rebels. During court interviews in 1863, for example, Confederate general Roswell Ripley recalled no fewer than seventeen duels fought among his fellow officers between 1845 and 1863, naming each combatant and their second off the top of his head.[157]

Even as early as 1806, the Articles of War (established under the U.S. War Department) had strictly forbidden all duelist activities. In fact, the articles were again revised in 1863 to read:

> ART. 25. *No officer or soldier shall send a challenge to another officer or soldier, to fight a duel, or accept a challenge if sent, upon pain, if a commissioned officer, of being cashiered; if a non-commissioned officer or soldier, of suffering corporeal punishment, at the discretion of a court-martial. ART. 26. IF any commissioned or non-commissioned officer commanding a guard shall knowingly or willingly suffer any person whatsoever to go forth and fight a duel, he shall be punished as a challenger, and all seconds, promoters, and carriers of challenges, in order to duels, shall be deemed principles, and be punished accordingly.*[158]

Unfortunately, these were regulations of the *United States*, not the newfound Confederacy, and dueling within the Southern ranks was as alive as ever. Thus, incredibly, dozens if not hundreds of Confederate military duels *a l'outrance* (to the death) occurred. Worse still, whether because of military training or battlefield experiences, duels among the upper ranks could at times be quite aggressive and produce devastating outcomes. Confederate major general John S. Marmaduke, for instance, dueled on the banks of the Arkansas River with fellow general Lucien M. Walker and killed him with multiple shots from his Colt revolver in 1863.[159]

Arguably the best case in point was a local yet extremely indiscreet affair of honor that happened in the midst of the Civil War and just before things in Charleston took a dramatic turn for the worse. Although a symbolic duel of the Confederacy, its outcome proved a monstrous distraction for high-ranking officers and even the Confederate States president himself. Nevertheless, when examined from a historical perspective, the fight between Alfred Moore Rhett and William Ransom Calhoun represented all that was right with dueling and all that was wrong with it when carried out in wartime.

Ransom Calhoun, a West Point graduate, and Alfred Rhett, a rice planter with a Harvard education, knew well the strife that had existed between their two families ever since the tariff crisis of 1842. Rhett's father, Robert Barnwell Rhett, and Calhoun's uncle, U.S. vice president John C. Calhoun, had argued bitterly at how best to handle the matter, and tensions remained heated for years afterward.

As for Ransom and Alfred, their relationship seemed to spiral downward from the very beginning. Both officers in the First South Carolina Artillery Battalion at the start of the war, the two consistently found themselves at odds. As Rhett's superior at Fort Moultrie in the days leading up to the firing on Fort Sumter, Calhoun frequently bypassed Rhett's command, issuing orders directly to Rhett's soldiers and even going so far as criticizing Rhett's lack of discipline after the bombardment's commencement.[160]

Barely one year later, Rhett and Calhoun were back together in Charleston, this time defending Fort Sumter itself from the Union navy's onslaught. Almost from the minute Calhoun arrived, Rhett was disgusted with him. Seamlessly picking up the squabble where they left off, Calhoun repeatedly questioned Rhett's handling of Sumter's defenses, while Rhett fueled dubious rumors concerning Colonel Calhoun's loyalty to the Confederate cause. After a while, both Calhoun and Rhett began voicing their grievances publicly around Charleston, and the once private hatred between the two finally erupted in the summer of 1862.

On the evening of August 7, a conversation at the Charleston Club between Rhett and Captain Arnoldus Vanderhorst turned ugly. At first, the two cordially debated the issue of who should replace Rhett's friend, Captain Thomas Wagner, who had been tragically killed a few weeks before by an accidental ordnance explosion inside Fort Moultrie. Vanderhorst suggested to Rhett that a West Point graduate might be a suitable candidate for the job, but Rhett immediately rebutted him, declaring, "A graduation at West Point was no guarantee of a good officer. I have known many who were not worth a damn. Moreover, my own experience in West Point men has been rather unfortunate."[161]

Perhaps innocently (but certainly inevitably), Vanderhorst mentioned Calhoun's name as a possible replacement for Wagner, suggesting that he was indeed a "fine officer" and a favorite of General Pierre Beauregard. Vanderhorst's compliment of Calhoun only infuriated Rhett, who crossly replied that he

did not care a damn what General Beauregard's or General Johnson's or anybody else's opinion might be concerning Colonel Ransom Calhoun.

A silk banner of William Ransom Calhoun's First Company (A), Battalion of Artillery, which was part of the garrison positioned at Fort Moultrie in the early stages of the Civil War. Alfred Rhett also served in this battalion as a major. *Courtesy of the Charleston Museum.*

[The man is] *not only no officer—my opinion of Colonel Calhoun is that he is a damned puppy. If you see anything personal yourself in what I have said, you are at liberty to take it as you please. My opinion is that Colonel Calhoun is a damned puppy.*[162]

Taken aback by Rhett's harshness, Vanderhorst made it known that he intended to disclose Rhett's words to Calhoun himself. Furthermore, having been on the receiving end of Rhett's tirade, Vanderhorst believed he *himself* insulted and asked Rhett to apologize. Rhett naturally refused, insisting that he meant what he said, thus opening the door to a challenge from Vanderhorst and subsequent duel.

Not long after Rhett and Vanderhorst fought without incident on August 9, Calhoun learned of Rhett's insults toward him, as well as Vanderhorst's duel in his defense. Incensed, Calhoun put forth his own challenge to Rhett on September 3:

> Major ALFRED RHETT:
> You have on many occasions assailed me with a view to injure my character, and under circumstances which gave me the right to demand redress. Influenced solely by considerations of public duty, I have hitherto waived my right. Persisting this course, you have lately in the presence of several gentlemen, used towards me offensive language which admits to no explanation. I now demand that satisfaction which is useful amongst gentlemen. My friend, Col O.M. Dantzler will make the necessary arrangements.
> Your Obdt. Servant, W.R. Calhoun[163]

On September 5, Alfred Rhett faced off against his Confederate rival Ransom Calhoun at Charleston's Oaks Club. The terms of the duel were read and agreed upon by both seconds, Olin M. Dantzler for Calhoun and Irvine K. Furman for Rhett:

> Terms of the meeting between Col. W.R. Calhoun and Major Alfred Rhett.
> 1st.   Time—Friday, the 5th September at 5 o'clock, P.M.
> 2d.   Place—Charleston Oaks Club.
> 3d.   Dress—The usual costume of a gentlemen, or uniform.
> 4th.   Weapons—the smooth-bore duelling [sic] pistol.
> 5th.   Distance—ten paces or thirty feet.
> 6th.   The pistol to be held perpendicularly with the muzzle down
> 7th.   The mode of giving he word shall be: "Gentlemen, prepare to receive the word!" "Are you ready!" "Fire—one, two, three—Halt!" The Pistols shall not be moved before the word, "fire," nor fired after the word, "Halt!"
> 8th.   On the ground the seconds shall toss up for choice of position, and the one losing the position shall have the word.
> 9th.   Each party shall have the privilege of having with him two friends and a Surgeon, in addition to his second.[164]

Once the two were in position, the word to fire was announced. Calhoun shot only a split second before Rhett but missed. Rhett's shot fared better and struck Calhoun in the chest, killing him.

Immediately, the consequences of the officers' duel reverberated all over Charleston. Making matters worse was the fact that Rhett was on active duty

6   The terms of meeting

Charleston Sept 4th 1862.

Terms of a meeting between Col W. R. Calhoun, and Major Alfred C Rhett.

1st Time   Friday the 5th of Sept at 5 ock P.m.

2d Place   Charleston, Oaks Club

3d Dress   The usual costume of a gentleman, or uniform

4th Weapon   The smooth bore Duelling pistol

5th Distance Ten paces or thirty feet

6th The Pistol to be held perpendicularly with muzzle down

7th The mode of giving the words shall be. "Gentlemen prepare to receive
    the word" Are you ready "Fire" One, two three Halt The pistol
    shall not be moved before the word "Fire" nor fired after the word Halt

8th On the ground the seconds shall toss up for the choice of position, and
the one losing the position shall have the word.

9th Each party shall have the privilege of having with him two friends
and a Surgeon in addition to his second.

                        Pm Dantzler   for Col W R Calhoun
                        I K Furman   for Major Alfred C Rhett

7   The statement of the seconds of the parties as to the conduct of the duel

        Statement of occurences on the field in the difficulty between Col
W. R. Calhoun and Major Alfred Rhett. The challenger with his friends and
r reb on the ground twenty minutes before 5 oclock and found the challenger
with his friends

A court document detailing the terms of the duel between Ransom Calhoun and Alfred
Rhett. *Courtesy of the Charleston Museum.*

while dueling a senior officer. Thus, a court of inquiry assembled to begin the laborious task of wading through witness after witness trying to get a handle on just what happened leading up to Calhoun's death and whether or not Rhett should be cashiered. For weeks the trial carried on with officials wondering just what they were supposed to do. Yes, Rhett had acted foolishly, but was it really illegal within the Confederate States army? Even the court documents themselves questioned the real necessity of going forth with the court of inquiry: "It is brought to the knowledge of the court that many duels, fatal and otherwise, have been fought between officers of the Confederate army, and of the old United States army, and that they have not been subjected to courts martial, nor dismissed [from] service…in any case specified within the memory of man."[165]

General Pierre Beauregard, meanwhile (perhaps wondering if he were the only one in town still aware of the war going on), was left with little choice but to intervene. Obviously, he needed his officers on duty and not withering away in some courtroom. Capitalizing on the War Department's hesitation, Beauregard fired off a rather direct letter to the war departments of South Carolina, Georgia and Florida on December 12, 1862. In it, he made his opinions perfectly clear that it was time to get back to the real fight:

> *While I deplore the unfortunate and untimely death of an accomplished, gallant soldier…I can only consider whether the interests and the good of the service require further proceedings to be had against that adversary, Major Alfred Rhett, for having accepted, in violation of the 25th Article of War, a challenge and fought a duel with another officer. Duelling [sic] among officers…has never been seriously noticed, and still less punished by the military authorities since the first enactment of the Article in 1776 or '7…[It] has always been a dead letter. It has never been carried into effect, and cannot be among men who on all occasions are ever ready to sacrifice rank and commission to preserve their honor.*[166]

Beauregard eventually heard back from the secretary of war, George W. Randolph, who, after discussing the matter with Jefferson Davis, decided that it was in the Confederate government's best interest to disown the whole mess. Randolph subsequently sent the entire issue back to Beauregard, leaving it to him to decide Rhett's fate. Amazingly, by January 13, 1863, Beauregard had not only arranged for Rhett's full pardon but also promoted him the new commander of Fort Sumter.

Even though Beauregard's authority and ultimate intervention helped sway the outcome of Alfred Rhett's trial, this kind of complete vindication was by no means unique. From the colonial period onward, local courts only seldom took the time to hear dueling trials, and even when they did, they were reluctant to prosecute simply on grounds of ritual and tradition. Juries were even more difficult to persuade. After their 1867 duel, police arrested Theodore C. Boag for killing Edward Roe, taking him and both seconds into custody and charging all three with murder. The jury disagreed with the prosecution's efforts and set everyone free after about fifteen minutes.[167]

To be sure, the disaster that was the Civil War affected the Lowcountry on a massive scale. The great fire of 1861, the incredibly lengthy siege by Federal artillery and the eventual occupation of Charleston by Union troops provided a series of devastating and demoralizing shockwaves. From these no one was immune. The city lay decimated at war's end, with most of its residents flat broke, homeless or both.

Thus, it is easy to think that with the devastation and overwhelming loss of life after the war, dueling would have become an obsolete practice not by public demand per se but, rather, for lack of people willing and able to indulge in it. Surely most southern soldiers returning from battle had washed off enough blood or heard enough gunfire that they no longer felt a need to prove their character nor wished to risk their lives any more than they had already.

Unfortunately, this was not so. While this notion of war-famished lads throwing down their arms for good certainly makes sense, there somehow remained that stubborn duelist's heritage that southern men—defeated or not—still chose to maintain.

Chapter 10

DOOMING THE DUELIST

Francis W. Dawson and a Farewell to Fighting

On September 30, 1812, around the same time the state legislature was taking up its first casual resolutions against dueling, the funeral of Mr. William Bay occurred in Charleston. In attendance was John Blake White, a friend of the deceased, who wrote in his journal some days later of the sadness, turmoil and ultimate loss caused by the hotheaded duelists:

> *The friends & fathers of these young men were acquainted with this intended duel before it took place. My heart bled this evening during the performance of the funeral ceremony to behold the venerable father, while he listened to the minister when he committed the body to the earth, "earth to earth, ashes to ashes, dust to dust." There was an immense concourse of people at the funeral, there were many eyes overflowing with tears. His venerable parents followed his remains to the grave, witnessed [their son] consigned to the bosom of the earth, heard the earth closing forever upon him, and the feelings of the father burst forth in loud, articulate sobs.[168]*

Under the early laws of proprietary Charles Towne, punishment for most violent acts was swift and hard. Circa 1710, in fact, crimes of murder under the English Statutes of Force plainly dictated that those convicted of such were to be either hanged or "marked with an M upon the brawn of the left thumb." The mark (as it was so politely called) was, in fact, the result of a red-hot iron brand administered by the town gaoler at court.[169]

To those in political authority during this period, duels—fatal ones anyway—seemed to fit nicely under the umbrella of murder. But dueling, to most who understood the tradition, was *not* murder or manslaughter—not even when one or both of its contestants died. For Charleston's gentry, dueling and crime simply did not equate. Its practice was a tradition outside the bounds of right and wrong. It was instead a defensive maneuver to ward off stigma and hence escape becoming a man of diminished virtue. Because of its detailed nature and steep heritage rooted in ancestral Europe, dueling had an uncanny ability for always squeezing in somewhere between the lines of what was or was not legal.

Alongside special committees and other organizations throughout the nineteenth century, groups of South Carolina policymakers tried and tried again to subdue dueling, putting forth legislation six different times in hopes of snuffing it out. State officials did their best to administer further updates and revisions to the lukewarm laws of 1812, revisiting the dueling argument every decade until the 1880s.

In 1823, for example, even with John Lyde Wilson in the middle of his term as governor, the state drafted the first of several amendments to the 1812 law and actually passed it some months later. This revised edition, while not drastically changing the original statute, made room for immunity in exchange for testimony in open court: "Any person concerned therein, either as a principal or second, or as counseling, aiding and abetting in such duel, shall give evidence against the person or persons actually indicted, without [in]criminating himself, or subjecting or making himself liable to any prosecution."[170]

Notwithstanding his personal beliefs, and knowing full well that proper gentlemen would never allow themselves to become turncoats, Governor Wilson signed the bill—likely with his tongue planted firmly in his cheek.

Some years later in 1834, the general assembly again revisited the anti-dueling juggernaut with still more alterations and amendments to the already existing "act to prevent the pernicious practice of Duelling [*sic*]." The bill—passed on December 17—did its best to motivate witnesses, offering them "one-half of the fine" collected from the convicted parties. It did not succeed. Dueling was, as it had always been, a gentlemanly rite sheltered from public scrutiny. Thus, finding anyone willing to give testimony condemning a duelist was immensely difficult, to say the least. Furthermore, in near total spite of having full knowledge of this updated law, Wilson published his dueling codes barely four years later, further exemplifying the complete futility of this latest anti-dueling movement.[171]

Dreadfully, dueling in South Carolina continued even after the Civil War, but thanks to fights like Boag-Roe and Rhett-Cooley, postwar duels were nearly impossible to keep secret. Thus, the anti-duelist movement forced the general assembly back to the drawing board in 1868 and again in 1873. Then, in December 1880, the lawmakers got it right.

In that year, the state finally put a decidedly harsh end to dueling in South Carolina. Law enforcement officials at long last received near carte-blanche liberty in taking down duelists and seconds alike, instituting fines and prison time for anyone even remotely involved in a planned duel. More drastically, amendments to section seven of chapter 128 within the state's general statutes introduced the death penalty for killing an opponent in a duel:

> *And in case any person shall kill another in any duel with a deadly weapon, or shall inflict a wound or wounds upon any person in a duel, so as person or persons so wounded shall thereof die within the space of six months then next following, that such person so killing another, or so wounding any person or persons so wounded shall due as aforesaid, being thereof convicted, shall suffer death as in the case of willful murder.*[172]

So why, after so many efforts before 1880 failed, was this final movement against dueling successful? The timing was good, for one thing, since the tragedy of the Cash-Shannon affair from earlier that year was still fresh in the minds of many. Consequently, more concentrated and aggressive anti-dueling charges were getting their long-overdue attention.

Fueled by the terrible conclusion of Cash-Shannon, the editor of Charleston's *News and Courier*, Francis Warington Dawson, decided that he for one had finally had enough. In fact, not just in 1880 but throughout the entire postbellum period prior, no duelist in Charleston or anywhere else in the state had a bigger enemy than Dawson (including opposing duelists). Dawson himself was a remarkable man, and given his background, it is a bit surprising he spent so much of his career arguing *against* the dueling tradition.

Born in England on May 20, 1840, Dawson was educated, well traveled and stood to inherit his father's wealth, making him a man of upstanding repute within the London elite. That was until the family fortune was lost and a rich aunt died, leaving him out of the will. Despite his misfortunes though, at least they happened at the right time. On December 20, 1860, South Carolina seceded from the United States, followed soon after by several other states. Four months later, soldiers in Charleston shelled Fort Sumter. Thus, the war in America called to Dawson's rich notions of adventure.

DUELLING DEAD IN CAROLINA.

THE PHILOSOPHY OF A PERSONAL DIFFICULTY IN COLUMBIA.

Dawson's anti-dueling crusade finally came to fruition in 1880 after the state legislature passed new and extremely tough laws against dueling and all its participants. *Courtesy of the Charleston Museum.*

Embarking for the newly established Confederate States of America in the winter of 1862, his fight was on from the very beginning.

Securing passage from England aboard the *Nashville*, a CSA-funded steamship bound for Morehead City, North Carolina, the twenty-year-old Dawson gained keen knowledge of seafaring tactics and defenses. Actually, he had to. From the moment Dawson's vessel set sail from Southampton, it was pursued by at least one other Federal gunboat all the way across the Atlantic and was forced to evade the Union blockade anchored off Cape Lookout. Despite the tense voyage, however, Dawson thrived. By the end of his trip, he was in the crew's good graces, as well as the captain's.[173]

The Confederate States navy commissioned Dawson—recommended by the *Nashville*'s captain as a hard worker and quick learner—to duty aboard a floating battery serving riverfront defenses near Richmond. After a brief and boring stint on the James River, however, Dawson left in search of more excitement. He soon found it, and by war's end, he was lucky to be alive. Dawson received a severe leg wound from enemy artillery at Mechanicsville in 1862 and barely three months later was captured near Sharpsburg, where he remained in custody for three weeks at Fort Delaware. In all, Dawson saw action in eleven different battles—Gettysburg and the Battle of the Wilderness among them—and was wounded on three separate occasions.[174]

Despite his valiant service to the Confederate cause, Dawson (like so many other Southern officers) was broke after the Confederate defeat, having "only five dollars, and a postage stamp to his name." Near penniless and jobless, the ever-ambitious Dawson pressed on with his new post-military life in America. He made friends easily and, more importantly, quickly. One of these was an experienced newspaperman named Bartholomew Rochefort Riorden, who befriended Dawson in 1866. After some months, and a little

Francis Warington Dawson, circa 1880, editor of the *News and Courier*. *Courtesy of the* Post and Courier.

convincing on Riorden's part, the duo headed to Charleston, where Riorden had once made a subtle name for himself with the *Charleston Mercury* during the war. Purchasing a one-third stake in the *Charleston Daily News*, Riorden and Dawson (who had to borrow his entire purchasing share for the buy-in) went to work.[175]

Together, Dawson and Riorden turned the deeply indebted *Daily News* into a powerful and formidable publication. Having rejuvenated both their newspaper and themselves by 1870, the paper was well circulated and consistently managed to turn a profit even in the throes of a downtrodden, postwar economy. In 1873, the *Daily News* purchased rival paper the *Charleston Courier* shortly after the death of its editor, Richard Yeadon, and on April 7, Dawson and Riorden printed the first edition of Charleston's *News and Courier.*

If nothing else, Dawson had a knack for editorials, and the soldier-turned-editor was brilliant at using his newspaper as a weapon. With his pen, Dawson railed against just about everything sinful, from whiskey to gambling to lynching, but he was especially outspoken on the dueling issue. For this, he certainly had his reasons. In the prewar years, Dawson himself had served as a second in four duels or more and had reportedly even issued a few challenges himself. Moreover, it was widely known around town that his own brother-in-law actually died fighting one.[176]

With the help of Dawson's fervent convictions, the Cash-Shannon affair was the last straw for duelists in the court of public opinion. Newspapers throughout the state, in fact, were quick to take the side of the deceased Shannon, defending him as a victim and indicting Cash as a homicidal maniac. Even the *New York Times* spared no effort in maligning Cash and his son, stating in the July 11, 1880 edition that the pair "hounded [Shannon] with the express purpose of murdering the old man in cold blood."

Despite his past as a hardened soldier somewhat used to violence and death, Dawson launched a vigorous anti-dueling campaign that for five months in 1880 rallied the anti-duelist collective. On July 7, just two days after Shannon was killed, Dawson printed his first of many editorials in the *Courier* calling out the ridiculousness of dueling:

> *We cast no stones at those who consider "The Code" a necessity or a shield, although, in our judgment, it is morally wrong and socially indefensible. How impotent it is! How vain it is! Once again he who was conceived to have done the wrong goes unscathed, and he who was sinned against lies dead, with a bullet in his noble, generous heart...We are confident that*

public opinion will sustain the demand that the law be enforced against everyone connected with the challenges, and the duel…Unless this is done, ceremonious manslaughter is no crime in South Carolina, and the laws against duelling [sic] *may as well be stricken from the statute book.*

Indeed, Dawson's pro-peace efforts were remarkable, and his editorial sincerity eventually helped sway a majority of opinions. His passions even caught the attention in 1883 of Pope Leo XIII, who knighted him a chevalier in the Order of St. Gregory the Great.

Of course, Dawson's story would have been much better had he lived a long life all the while fighting the good fight of the righteous. Sadly, this was not to be. What took place on the afternoon of March 12, 1889, remains unclear even to this day, but whatever happened, Dawson was dead before nightfall—killed by an acquaintance, Dr. Thomas B. McDow.

After learning of an alleged love affair between his children's governess, twenty-two-year-old Helene Marie Burdayron, and McDow, a married man, Dawson was enraged. Like all things unholy, Dawson viewed adultery as a reprehensible crime and sought out McDow to put an end to the inappropriate relationship. Upon barging through McDow's office door, the two were overheard arguing by a nearby stagecoach driver. At some point during the row, McDow fired a pistol at Dawson, killing him.

Curiously, however, McDow was slow to notify the police, doing so only after several hours of trying to hide Dawson's body beneath the basement floorboards. Failing to do a suitable job of concealing the evidence, McDow moved Dawson's body back to the room where he had shot him. Only then did he notify authorities.[177]

After his arrest, McDow would later testify:

[Dawson] *struck me a staggering blow on the chest which caused me to fall back over my lounge and strain my back. I endeavored to get up, and while struggling to do so Captain Dawson gave me a cut across my head with a cane, indenting my hat and causing me to stagger again. While trying to recover myself, and seeing him in the act of aiming another blow at me with his cane, I managed to get around to my desk and get my pistol.*[178]

Regardless of these claims of self-defense, McDow went to trial for Dawson's murder. Yet without any credible eyewitnesses, the prosecution had little to go on. The jury promptly returned a not guilty verdict, acquitting McDow on all charges.

CAPT DAWSON MURDERED.

THE NEWS THAT SHOCKED ALL CHARLESTON LAST NIGHT.

Killed Early in the Afternoon by Dr T. B. McDow in the Office of the Latter—The Murderer Remains Locked Up with the Body of his Victim for Two Hours—An Attempt at Secret Burial—Failure and Subsequent Surrender to the Police— The Cause of the Crime.

Capt Francis Warrington Dawson, the editor and manager of The News and Courier, ended a most brilliant career yesterday afternoon about 4 o'clock, having been slain almost in sound of the voices the dearest to him on earth. This cold, bare recital of the event fails to convey, nor can, perhaps, any relation convey, an adequate idea of the thrill of horror which stirred this whole community when the story of the deed was bruited on the streets. There was none in Charleston, from the humblest to the highest, to whom either the name or the man was not intimately known. No wonder, then, that the story of the murder should have gone like an electric current of information

News of Dawson's murder in 1889 spread quickly throughout Charleston and the rest of the eastern United States. His killer's trial that followed was one of the hottest topics of the decade. *Courtesy of the* Post and Courier.

Second Edition.

SUNDAY, JUNE 30—4 A. M.

ON TRIAL FOR HIS LIFE.

DR McDOW ACQUITTED OF THE MURDER OF CAPT DAWSON.

The Last Scenes in the Tragedy of March 12—Major Julian Mitchell's Magnificent Address to the Jury—Dr McDow's Friends Congratulate him on his Escape.

There was a distinctive feature in the surroundings at the Court House yesterday. On Friday the distinguished counsel for the accused had had the whole day to themselves, and while the crowd was large it was composed principally of those who had followed the case from the start, with a desire doubtless to see and hear all that was to be seen and heard. Apparently, the most interested part of the audience during the trial were the colored people, who regularly occupied the southern half of that portion of the Court room which is supposed to be reserved for the public. They were there every day, always promptly, and they stayed to the end. They were in their places yesterday, and they saw the case out to the end.

Dr. Thomas B. McDow, on trial for the murder of Francis W. Dawson, claimed self-defense and was soon after found not guilty for lack of any eyewitness testimony. *Courtesy of the Charleston Museum.*

Thanks in large part to Francis Dawson, proper dueling died away in South Carolina, and dueling among Charlestonians grew fainter with each passing year after 1880. Not to suggest it disappeared entirely though. In truth, quarreling, nastiness and overall combativeness among southerners was far from finished, and as America expanded westward during the late 1880s and '90s, whatever was left of controlled, civilized and sophisticated gunfights effortlessly morphed into haphazard, lawless saloon-style showdowns.

Gone were the days of the formal duel a la Gadsden-Howe or Hamilton-Burr, leaving only loutish and uncultured brawls to fill the void. To muck things up even more, frontiersmen heading west seemingly had no trouble abandoning all forms of antebellum tradition. Even dueling's purists eventually conceded that cordial combat had become brutal murder by the mid-1890s and consequently discarded their once earnest belief in the code of honor.

One horrific example of this deterioration was the fabled "Missouri Duel" first introduced (probably invented) in Mexico by General Joseph Orville Shelby's regiment of Missouri Volunteers, who had fled the country after the Confederate surrender. Deeming firearms as perhaps too impersonal, Shelby's unique rules called for two adversaries to connect themselves physically by way of a red bandanna, each clinching a corner between his front teeth. Once in position, the two proceeded to slash away at each other with Bowie knives until someone released the bandana, thus accepting defeat.[179]

In Charleston, dueling remained a hot-button topic for years after the 1880 state legislation. For as many individuals, special-interest groups, church committees and newspapers that raged against it, there seemed to be just as many wishing to reinstate it. Were they wrong? Well, for lack of a better word, duels *worked*—or appeared to at least when judged against the post-dueling days of the 1880s, '90s and early 1900s. Shockingly, a mere ten years after the formal ban on dueling, South Carolina's homicide rate skyrocketed, tripling that of all New England states combined. This dreadful spike in crime in and around Charleston did not go unnoticed among the citizens, as one Charles Drayton opined:

> *The best way to prevent any street fights is to abolish that miserable anti-dueling law. Get Governor Lyde Wilson's Code of Honor and you will find that he claims in the preface that its intention is to save human life. Fatal duels were the exception, and horrible as was the occasional loss of life, it was not as bad as the present murderous street fights which I consider the*

legitimate outcome of the anti-dueling law. Outsiders may clamor as they please about the barbarity of the Code Duello, but hundreds of God-fearing men and church members still believe in it. It makes men respect themselves and their fellows more than they do now, and it required satisfaction for insults or slighting remarks to women, which no amount of damages recovered in a circuit court could equal in the mind of an honorable man.[180]

Unlike coldblooded murder, maybe dueling's rituals deserve a *little* credit. It is hard to argue that dueling, for all its flaws, was at least organized and, to a degree, manageable. Years later, in fact, reminiscences of the duel's value in Charleston were evident within public discussion:

One who can remember the exquisite urbanity of the social intercourse of fifty years ago, and contrast it with the careless expressions, the rough give and take, of the present, can but wonder how much the old way had to do with the self-respect and consideration for others of that society which people now call half civilized. At its worst—and its worst was very grievous—dueling was not so bad as those shocking unregulated encounters which occur now when the passions of men are beyond control, and which cost more lives than were ever sacrificed to the old duello.[181]

For better or worse, the art of dueling is gone now, but who's to say it cannot make some sort of crackpot comeback? Nowadays, just mentioning pistol dueling (especially among those disinterested in history) makes for a laughable anecdote, a good story to share at the pub and usually nothing more. Nevertheless, the *idea* of dueling is still very much alive, and its values stretch far and wide outside state lines still today.

In the fall of 2002, for example, with tensions between the Unites States and Iraq running extremely high over Saddam Hussein's rumored weapons stockpiles, Iraq's vice president, Taha Yassin Ramadan, recommended a duel between his president Hussein and U.S. president George W. Bush. The suggested fight was to take place in a neutral territory complete with seconds, surgeons and matching weapons, be they pistols, swords or whatever. Needless to say, Yassin's offer was thoroughly rebuked, and the United States went to war with Iraq (again) in 2003.[182]

Here at home, South Carolina's practicing attorneys and peace officers continued to swear oaths respecting the state's anti-dueling statutes for decades after 1880. The latter even took an entirely separate pledge before witnesses that "I will to the extent of my ability, enforce the penalties prescribed by law against dueling, and will not fail to bring to justice all persons offending against the said law that may come within my view of knowledge."[183]

Moreover, the following passage is still included in the oath administered to Kentucky's secretaries of state: "I do further solemnly swear [or affirm] that since the adoption of the present Constitution, I, being a citizen of this State, have not fought a duel with deadly weapons within this State nor out of it."[184]

Finally, as a testament to South Carolina's dueling heritage, the state to this day expressly lists dueling as a capital crime separate from murder. Under chapter three of title sixteen in the South Carolina Code of Laws remains article five, the dueling law:

> SECTION 16-3-410. Sending or accepting challenge to fight.
> It is unlawful for a person to challenge another to fight with a sword, pistol, rapier, or any other deadly weapon or to accept a challenge. A person who violates the provisions of this section is guilty of a misdemeanor and, upon conviction, must be imprisoned not more than two years. A person convicted under this section is deprived of the right of suffrage, and is disabled from holding any office of honor or trust in this State.
> SECTION 16-3-420. Carrying or delivering challenge; serving as second.
> Whoever shall (a) willingly or knowingly carry or deliver any such challenge in writing or verbally deliver any message intended as, or purporting to be, such a challenge, (b) be present at the fighting of any duel as a second or (c) aid or give countenance thereto shall, for every such offense, on conviction thereof, be forever disabled from holding any office of honor or trust in this State and shall be imprisoned in the Penitentiary for a term not exceeding two years, at the discretion of the court, and shall be fined in a sum not less than five hundred dollars nor more than one thousand dollars.[185]

It seems silly to some and superfluous to others, but in fact, the law as written is very much alive and strictly enforced—even now. On September 2, 2009, the Charleston Police Department charged a man with dueling after allegedly killing an adversary of his. Reportedly, the pair agreed to fight it out with pistols in the middle of the street near the corner of King and Simons. Naturally, this duel sorely lacked such formalities as dress codes, seconds, smoothbore muzzleloaders and a holy host of other indemnities. However, because "the suspect challenged the victim to go get a gun," a duel is therefore the result in the eyes of South Carolina's current law.[186]

CHARLESTON SHOOTING

Police charge man with killing in a duel

BY PRENTISS FINDLAY
The Post and Courier

Darnell Tyrell White challenged Kevin Lamar "Curly" Johnson to a duel on Sept. 2, Charleston police said Wednesday.

After they exchanged several shots, Johnson lay mortally wounded next to a dumpster near the corner of King and Simons streets, according to police.

"The suspect challenged the victim to go get a gun. It just es-

calated from there," said Charleston Police Public Information Officer Charles Francis.

Charleston Police and the U.S. Marshals Service arrested White without incident on Tuesday night at a Dorchester Road motel. White, 25, of 3429 Osceola St., was being held at the Charleston County Detention Center on Wednesday where he was awaiting a bail hearing. White is charged with killing in a duel, Francis said.

Johnson, 29, was shot several times behind 1106 King St. at

about 7:30 p.m. on Sept. 2. Witnesses told police that they heard an argument and then gunfire. Johnson was dead at the scene from multiple gunshot wounds. Johnson, a plumber's assistant, was riding his bike at the time of the shooting.

The violence rattled neighborhood residents who said that they heard what sounded like two shots from a .38-caliber pistol and automatic weapons fire. Francis said he could not discuss why the gunfight happened, citing the ongoing

investigation.

Johnson's family has said that he dreamed of opening a bicycle rental shop downtown. Area residents have said he carried his son, Jamir Johnson, 2, on his bike handlebars when riding around the area.

Anyone with information can call Charleston Police at 577-7434 or Crime Stoppers at 554-1111.

Reach **Prentiss Findlay** at 937-5711 or pfindlay@postandcourier.com

Title sixteen, chapter three, article five of South Carolina's law codes still lists dueling as a crime separate from murder and is presently enforced as such, as in the charging of a man in 2009 with killing in a duel. *Courtesy of the Charleston Museum.*

Of course, there will likely never be a realistic way of knowing *all* the duels that took place in South Carolina. Indeed, it is hard enough pinning down just those that occurred in Charleston. But maybe this is for the best. For locals, there were plenty of other opportunities throughout the eighteenth and nineteenth centuries to die: two enemy sieges and subsequent occupations, five major fires, horrid storms, myriad health woes (including repeated outbreaks of smallpox, cholera and yellow fever) and even an earthquake. Add to this list the countless deaths brought about by gentlemanly arguments that spiraled into fatal shootouts. Dueling, for as coarse and tragic as it was, was nevertheless a staple in the gentrified society of Charleston, and its legacy will forever remain an extraordinary aspect of southern social history.

NOTES

CHAPTER 1

1. Edgar, *South Carolina*, 50.
2. Fitzsimmons, "Hot Words."
3. Ramsay, *History of South-Carolina*, 388.
4. Faust, Weidmann and Wehner, "Influence of Meteorological Factors," 150–56; Rotton and Cohn,"Outdoor Temperature," 276–306.
5. Stephen West Moore, letter to son, October 15, 1823, "Letters, Notes, and Correspondences Concerning Dueling."
6. Lovell, *Golden Isles of Georgia*, 184–86.
7. Fitzsimmons, "Hot Words."
8. As famous as Hamilton's death was at the hands of Aaron Burr, it's easy to forget that Hamilton's nineteen-year-old son, Philip, also died in a previous duel with George Eacker on November 23, 1801—on the very same field where his father faced Burr a few years later.
9. Dr. Howard Kurtzman, in discussion with the author, September 2011.
10. Shakespeare, *Tragedy of Troilus and Cressida*, act V, sc. 3.
11. Andre, "Duel between General Howe and General Gadsden."
12. Godbold and Woody, *Christopher Gadsden*, 186.
13. Fitzsimmons, "Hot Words."
14. "Becoming Carolinians," Charleston Museum, SC. August 23, 2000.
15. Simms, *History of South Carolina*, 128.
16. Edgar, *South Carolina*, 207.

17. Rogers, "Papers of James Grant," 146–48; Wallace, *Life of Henry Laurens*, 109.
18. Moultrie, *Memoirs of the American Revolution*, I: 119.
19. Greene, *Papers of General Nathanael Greene*, IX: 625.
20. Paullin, "Dueling in the Old Navy," 1156–197.

CHAPTER 2

21. *Random House Unabridged Dictionary*, "Duel."
22. Shakespeare and Andrews, *Antony and Cleopatra*, act 4 sc. 1.
23. Cooper and McCord, *Statutes at Large of South Carolina*, 272.
24. Fitzsimmons, "Hot Words."
25. Dunlop, "Letters from John Stewart to William Dunlop," 45.
26. Kellett, "Single Combat," 13, books.google.com/books?id=vIgo_Kspeo IC&pg=PA9&lpg=PA9&dq=kellett+single+combat.
27. The exact date of the contest between d'Eu and Baynard is unknown but was likely sometime in the eleventh century. As Sabine writes, it was one of the earliest wagers of battle to occur in England. Additionally, the *Domesday Book* reveals that the nature of d'Eu's mutilation included having his eyes gouged out and castration. Sabine, *Notes on Duels*, 1, 174.
28. Ibid., 1.
29. Kellett, "Single Combat," 14.
30. Neilson, *Trial by Combat*, 47, 157
31. Tocqueville, *Democracy in America*, II: 139–40.
32. Kaeuper, *Chivalry and Violence*, 141.
33. Sabine, *Notes on Duels*, 18–19; Hopkins, *Tournaments and Joust*, 7.
34. Robertson, *Works of William Robertson*, IV: 357–58.
35. Ibid., 63.
36. Twain, *Autobiography of Mark Twain*, I: 202.
37. Sabine, *Notes on Duels*, 6.
38. Ibid., 15.

CHAPTER 3

39. O'Driscoll will reprinted in Fitzsimmons, "Hot Words."
40. Quincy, *Memoir of Josiah Quincy Jun.*, 95.

41. Burton, *South Carolina Silversmiths*, xiv; Burton, *Charleston Furniture*, 6.
42. Tocqueville, *Democracy in America*, II: 138.
43. Royal Code reprinted in Hamilton, *Only Approved Guide*, 32.
44. *Charleston Mercury*, September 5–6, 1823.
45. Stephen West Moore, letter to son, October 15, 1823, "Letters, Notes, and Correspondences Concerning Dueling."
46. Fitzsimmons, "Hot Words."
47. Notes describing Timothy-Reed duel, 1794, "Letters, Notes, and Correspondences Concerning Dueling."
48. King, *Newspaper Press of Charleston*, 162–63.
49. Magruder, *History of Louisiana*, 353.
50. *South Carolina Gazette*, September 20, 1787.
51. Stevens, *Pistols at Ten Paces*, 82.
52. The same can be said for St. Michael's Alley connecting Church and Meeting Streets. Only one recorded swordfight took place here circa 1801 (see chapter eight).
53. Wright, *Edisto*, 49.
54. Byron, "Crime and Punishment," 92.

Chapter 4

55. Hamilton, *Only Approved Guide*, 3.
56. King, *Newspaper Press of Charleston*, 150.
57. The 1804 Hamilton-Burr duel occurring in Weehawken, New Jersey.
58. Fitzsimmons, "Hot Words."
59. Notes discussing Wilson-Middleton negotiations, 1824, "Letters, Notes, and Correspondences Concerning Dueling."
60. Wilson, *Code of Honor*, 21.
61. Ibid., 12.
62. Fitzsimmons, "Hot Words."
63. Wilson, *Code of Honor*, 33.
64. Unfortunately, Gough's involvement with duels was not over. He was shot and killed in one in the spring of 1836. His obituary in the May 19 *Courier* read, "Sad has been his lot and a melancholy warning to us all to endeavor to restrain our passions to exercise forbearance toward each other. Peace be to his Ashes."
65. Elzas, *Leaves from My Historical Scrapbook*.

66. Ibid.

67. Notes discussing Senter-Rutledge duel, "Letters, Notes, and Correspondences Concerning Dueling"; Rowland, Moore and Rogers, *History of Beaufort County*, I: 272–73.

68. Notes discussing Senter-Rutledge duel, "Letters, Notes, and Correspondences Concerning Dueling."

CHAPTER 5

69. Wilson, *Code of Honor*, 10.

70. *Code Duello*, rule 14.

71. *Code Duello*, rule 21; Wilson, *Code of Honor*, 13–14.

72. Fitzsimmons, "Hot Words"; notes discussing Quash-Simons duel, 1826, "Letters, Notes, and Correspondences Concerning Dueling."

73. "Letters, Notes, and Correspondences Concerning Dueling."

74. Sabine, *Notes on Duels*, 231; Fitzsimmons, "Hot Words."

75. Wilson, *Code of Honor*, 10.

76. Pistols equipped with "scratch rifling," or extremely thin and shallow grooves, appear from time to time, an alteration that is barely detectable to untrained eyes without good lighting.

77. Wilson, *Code of Honor*, 24.

78. Notes discussing Crafts-Bay duel, n.d., "Letters, Notes, and Correspondences Concerning Dueling"; Williams, *Dueling in the Old South*, 22.

79. Publicly shamed after the duel, Crafts left the state. "Letters, Notes, and Correspondences Concerning Dueling."

80. Wilson, *Code of Honor*, 20.

81. Cantey, *Edisto*, 49.

82. Ibid., 50–51.

CHAPTER 6

83. *City Gazette*, November 9, 1795, November 11, 1799, September 6, 1800.

84. Pollard, *History of Firearms*, 83.

85. Ibid., 87.

86. Ibid., 85–87.

87. Murray-Flutter, conversation with author, May 2003.

88. A pistol in the "snap" position sometimes referred to a half-cocked position, which will not fire. Failure to pull back the gun cock completely was the second's error.

89. Wilson, *Code of Honor*, 30.

90. The few witnesses to the 1812 Bay-Crafts duel from the previous chapter also maintained that Crafts, besides firing prematurely, took an unfair advantage by secretly equipping his pistol with a hair trigger, which was never part of the agreed terms. "Letters, Notes, and Correspondences Concerning Dueling."

91. These modifications remained undiscovered until the 1970s when, in observance of the United States Bicentennial celebrations, Italian gunsmith Walter Agnoletto analyzed the pistols for reproduction. Lindsay, "Pistols Shed Light," 94–97.

92. Murray-Flutter, conversation with author.

93. Shoemaker, "Taming of the Duel," 533.

94. Pollard, *History of Firearms*, 86–94.

95. Fitzsimmons, "Hot Words."

96. *News and Courier*, April 2, 1873.

97. *Savannah Daily Republican*, January 15, 1841; Duval County probate records (County Courthouse, Jacksonville, FL).

98. Wilson, *Code of Honor*, 19.

99. Duffy, *Rudolph Matas History of Medicine*, II; Matheny, conversation with author, October 26, 2011.

100. Petigru and Carson, *Life, Letters and Speeches of James Louis Petigru*, 65.

101. Ibid.

102. Ibid.

103. Ibid., 72.

CHAPTER 7

104. Fleming, "When Politics Was Not Only Nasty," 58.

105. Gregg and Dargan, *History of the Old Cheraws*, 395–98.

106. Caruthers and Craven, *History of Col. David Fanning*, 2.

107. Fitzsimmons, "Hot Words."

108. Fanning tried at least one more time to reclaim his horse after the war, unsuccessfully taking his case to court. Left with no other choice, Fanning

issued a challenge to Hunter. Had the war still been going on, however, Fanning could have just killed him without consequence. Notes describing Hunter-Fanning duel, n.d., "Letters, Notes, and Correspondences Concerning Dueling."

109. Wilson, *Code of Honor*, 20.

110. Rhett actually did accept a challenge from rival senator Daniel Elliott Huger in 1830. Rhett apologized the next day and thus avoided the contest. Reed, "Satisfaction Usual Among Gentlemen," 536.

111. Ladd, Haskins and Chittenden, *Literary Remains*, 227–28.

112. "Letters, Notes, and Correspondences Concerning Dueling"; Ladd, Haskins and Chittenden, *Literary Remains*, xxiv.

113. Some historians have said over time that it was not Isaac's intention to kill Ladd and that he purposely aimed low in an effort merely to wound him. This theory is suspect since the two were both using smoothbore pistols. Thus, targeting a leg at a distance of some fifteen to twenty yards and actually hitting it is a difficult feat to be sure. Also, even if Isaac meant to just wound Ladd, medical treatments of 1786 could in no way guarantee that a leg wound would be survivable.

114. Wilson, *Code of Honor*, 23.

115. Cumming McDuffie pamphlet p.2-4; Chas Mus. archives, SC CR4571

116. Adams, *John Quincy Adams*, VI: 77.

117. Cumming, *Cumming-McDuffie Duels*, 14; "Letters, Notes, and Correspondences Concerning Dueling."

118. Adams, *John Quincy Adams*, 76.

119. Cumming, *Cumming-McDuffie Duels*, 16.

120. Ibid., 22.

121. Sabine, *Notes on Duels*, 138; "Letters, Notes, and Correspondences Concerning Dueling."

122. Fitzsimmons, "Hot Words."

123. Keitt barely survived the massive Union siege of Battery Wagner in 1863, at one point even asking General Beauregard if he intended to "sacrifice the garrison" in its entirety. Notes discussing the Dantzler-Keitt duel, "Letters, Notes, and Correspondences Concerning Dueling"; Roman, *Military Operations of General Beauregard*, II: 132.

CHAPTER 8

124. Hartwell, "Study of Anatomy," 67–68.

125. Fleming, "When Politics Was Not Only Nasty," 58–59.

126. Brown, *Southern Honor*, 98–99.

127. Holland, *Gentlemen's Blood*, 200; Sabine, *Notes on Dueling*, 328.

128. Both Walter Edgar's *South Carolina, A History* (p. 306) and William Freehling's *Prelude to Civil War* (p. 150) cite Hamilton as a principal in fourteen duels. However, Tinkler's *James Hamilton of South Carolina* (p. 31) states that Hamilton likely fought in only one.

129. Tinkler, *James Hamilton*, 6.

130. Fraser, *Lowcountry Hurricanes*, 33–38.

131. Tinkler, *James Hamilton*, 26.

132. Behan, *Short History of Callawassie Island*, 49–53.

133. Tinkler, *James Hamilton*, 31.

134. Ibid., 61.

135. Waring, "Medicine in Charleston," 25.

136. Notes discussing the Haley-Delancey, "Letters, Notes, and Correspondences Concerning Dueling."

137. The Haley-Delancey and Placide-Douvilliers duels are what likely birthed the long-standing myth that St. Michael's Alley just south of the Meeting and Broad Street intersection was a widely used dueling lane among locals. These two fights appear to be the only recorded duels to have occurred there. Ibid.

138. Lee's loathing of Washington actually dated back to before the war, when he lost out to Washington for the initial command of the Continental army. Massey, *John Laurens*, 110–14.

139. Ibid., 125.

140. Ibid. Lee's second was Evan Edwards; Laurens's was none other than Alexander Hamilton.

141. Sabine, *Notes on Dueling*, 227–28.

142. Gamble, *Savannah Duels*, 260–67.

143. Sims and Marion-Sims, *Story of My Life*, 89.

144. Ibid., 90–91.

145. Truman, *Field of Honor*, 152–53; Zacks, *Underground Education*, 111.

Chapter 9

146. Bacon and Montagu, *Works of Francis Bacon*, II: 296.

147. Gilman, *Funeral Address*.

148. Weems, *God's Revenge Against Duelling*, quoted in Koerner, "Demanding Satisfaction."

149. Ibid.

150. Notes discussing anti-dueling movements in Charleston, "Letters, Notes, and Correspondences Concerning Dueling."

151. Ibid.

152. Fitzsimmons, "Hot Words."

153. Ibid.

154. Williams, *Dueling in the Old South*, 66; Fitzsimmons, "Hot Words."

155. Dueling instances among French military officers actually increased, especially in the waning years of Louis XIV's reign. Lynn, *Giant of the Grand Siècle*, 256–57; Sabine, *Notes on Dueling*, 9.

156. Calhoun, *Some Reminiscences*, 7.

157. "Papers Touching Interview of April 23, 1862," Files on Alfred Rhett, 1975.125, Archives Dept., Charleston Museum (Charleston), n.p.

158. United States War Department, *1863 Laws of War*, 9–10.

159. Steward, *Duels and the Roots of Violence*, 194–95; Horres, "Affair of Honor at Fort Sumter," 12.

160. Horres, "Affair of Honor at Fort Sumter," 14–18.

161. Court papers in relation to the duel between Captain Arnoldus Vanderhorst and Major Alfred Rhett, 1863, Files on Alfred Rhett, 1975.125, Archives Dept., Charleston Museum (Charleston).

162. In this period, referring to a man as a puppy implied that he was literally a son of a bitch. Fitzsimmons, "Hot Words."

163. "Papers Touching Interview," Files on Alfred Rhett, Charleston Museum.

164. Ibid.

165. Ibid.

166. Ibid.

167. Moore, *Carnival of Blood*, 12.

CHAPTER 10

168. Fitzsimmons, "Hot Words."

169. Cooper and McCord, *Statutes at Large of South Carolina*, 455.

170. "Letters, Notes, and Correspondences Concerning Dueling."

171. Fitzsimmons, "Hot Words."

172. Ibid.

173. Rowe, *Pages of History*, 57.

174. Ibid., 58.

175. Ibid.

176. Ibid., 62.

177. Moore, *Carnival of Blood*, 94.

178. *New York Times*, "Shot Without Warning, Atrocious Murder of Capt. F.W. Dawson," March 13, 1889.

179. Steward, *Duels and the Roots of Violence*, 197.

180. Fitzsimmons, "Hot Words"; Edgar, *South Carolina*, 417.

181. Ravenel, *Charleston*, 414–15.

182. Wallace, "W.H. Rejects Bush-Saddam Duel Offer."

183. Fitzsimmons, "Hot Words."

184. Kentucky Secretary of State, "Oath of Office," Secretary's Desk, www.sos.ky.gov/secdesk/history/oath.

185. South Carolina Legislature, "Code of Laws," South Carolina Law, www.scstatehouse.gov/code/t16c003.

186. *Post and Courier*, "Police Charge Man with Killing in a Duel," September 2, 2009, sec. B1.

Bibliography

Much information in this book came from newspapers printed in Charleston during the eighteenth and nineteenth centuries and is referenced within the text where applicable.

Adams, John Quincy. *John Quincy Adams in Russia, Comprising Portions of the Diary of John Quincy Adams from 1809 to 1814*. CT: Praeger, 1970.

Andre, John. "Duel between General Howe and General Gadsden." Charleston: (43/637) South Carolina Historical Society.

Apothecaries' Hall, a Unique Exhibit at the Charleston Museum; An Ancient Drug Store Whose Business Survived Plagues, Wars, Great Fires and Earthquakes for One Hundred and Forty Years. Its History Including Some Remarks upon the State of Pharmacy and Med. Archival reference, Charleston, SC: Presses of Southern Print. & Pub. Co., 1923.

Atkinson, John A. *The British Duelling Pistol*. Bloomfield, Ontario: Museum Restoration Service, 1978.

An Authentic Account of the Fatal Duel Fought on Sunday the 21ˢᵗ March 1860, Near Chester, Penna. between Mr. Charels G. Hunter, Late Midshipman of the U.S. Navy, and Mr. William Miller, Jun. Late Attorney at Law of Philadelphia Containing an Impartial. Washington City: Jonathan Elliot, bookseller, 1830.

Bacon, Francis, and Basil Montagu. *The Works of Francis Bacon, Lord Chancellor of England*. Philadelphia: Carey and Hart, 1844.

Bartlett, Robert. *Trial by Fire and Water: The Medieval Judicial Ordeal*. Oxford: Clarendon Press, 1986.

Behan, William A. *A Short History of Callawassie Island, South Carolina: The Lives and Times of Its Owners and Residents 1711–1985*. New York: iUniverse, 2004.

Bowers, Claude Gernade. *Jefferson and Hamilton: The Struggle for Democracy in America*. Boston: Houghton Mifflin Co., 1925.

The British Code of Duel: A Reference to the Laws of Honour and the Character of a Gentleman. Reprint by the Richmond Publishing Co., Ltd., 1971. London: Knight and Lacey, 1824.

Brown, Bertram. *Southern Honor: Ethics and Behavior in the Old South*. London: Oxford University Press, 1982.

Burton, E. Milby. *Charleston Furniture, 1700–1825*. Charleston, SC: Charleston Museum, 1955.

———. *South Carolina Silversmiths, 1690–1860*. Charleston, SC: Charleston Museum, 1968.

Byron, Matthew A. "Crime and Punishment: The Impotency of Dueling Laws in the United States." PhD thesis, Ann Arbor, MI, 2008.

Calhoun, Edwin. *Some Reminiscences of a Confederate Soldier: Edwin Calhoun, Company C, 6th South Carolina Calvary, Confederate States of America*. N.p., n.d.

Calhoun, William R., and Alfred Rhett. "Letters of Colonel W.R. Calhoun and Major Alfred Rhett." Charleston, SC: (1975.125) Charleston Museum Archives.

Carey, Mathew, and George McDuffie. "Look before You Leap: Addresses to the Citizens of the Southern States: Being a Solemn Warning against the Destructive Doctrine of a Separation of the Union, Advocated in the Late Message of His Excellency George M'Duffie." Philadelphia: Haswell & Barrington, 1834–1835.

Caruthers, E.W., and B. Craven. *A Brief History of Col. David Fanning: Also, Naomi Wise, or the Wrongs of a Beautiful Girl: and Randolph's Manufacturing.* Weldon, NC: Harrell's Printing House, 1888.

Cashin, Edward J. *William Bartram and the American Revolution on the Southern Frontier.* Columbia: University of South Carolina Press, 2000.

Conner, James. "Papers Relating to the Taber-Magrath Duel, 1856." Charleston: (247.00) South Carolina Historical Society.

Cooper, Thomas, and David James McCord. *The Statutes at Large of South Carolina.* Columbia: A.S. Johnston, 1836.

Cumming, Joseph. *The Cumming-McDuffie Duels.* Pamphlet, Savannah: Georgia Historical Society, 1960.

Cummins, Joseph. *Great Rivals in History: When Politics Gets Personal.* New York: Metro Books, 2008.

DeSaussure, Henry William. "Henry William DeSaissure Papers, 1795–1838." Charleston: (1022.02.02) South Carolina Historical Society.

Duffy, J. *The Rudolph Matas History of Medicine in Louisiana.* Baton Rouge: Louisiana State University Press for the Rudolph Matas Trust Fund, 1962.

Dunlop, J.G. "Letters from John Stewart to William Dunlop." *South Carolina Historical & Genealogical Magazine* 32 (1931): 45.

Edgar, Walter B. *South Carolina: A History.* Columbia: University of South Carolina Press, 1998.

Elzas, Barnett A. *Leaves from My Historical Scrapbook.* Charleston, 1908.

Faust, V., M. Weidmann and W. Wehner. "The Influence of Meteorological Factors on Children and Youths." *International Journal of Child & Adolescent Psychiatry* 40, no. 4 (1974): 150–56.

Findlay, Prentiss. "Police Charge Man with Killing in a Duel." *Post and Courier*, September 2, 2009: 1-B.

Fitzsimmons, Mabel Trott. "Hot Words and Hair Triggers." Charleston, SC: (F266 F112 394.8 Fi) Charleston Museum Archives, 1934.

Fleming, Thomas. "When Politics Was Not Only Nasty…But Dangerous." *American Heritage*, Spring 2011.

Flexner, Stuart Berg. *Random House Unabridged Dictionary*. 2nd ed. New York: Random House, 1993.

Forsyth, William, and Appleton Morgan. *History of Trial by Jury*. New York: J. Cockroft, 1875.

Fortier, Alcee. *A History of Louisiana*. New York: Goupil & Co. of Paris, Manzi, Joyant & Co. successors, 1904.

Fraser, Walter J. *Lowcountry Hurricanes: Three Centuries of Storms at Sea and Ashore*. Athens: University of Georgia Press, 2006.

Freehling, William W. *Prelude to Civil War: The Nullification Controversy in South Carolina*. 1st ed. New York: Harper & Row, 1966.

Freeman, Joanne B. *Affairs of Honor: National Politics in the New Republic*. New Haven, CT: Yale University Press, 2001.

Gamble, Thomas. *Savannah Duels and Duelists: 1733–1877*. Savannah, GA: Review Publishing and Printing Co., 1923.

Gilman, Samuel. *Funeral Address, Delivered at the Second Presbyterian Independent Church, Charleston (South Carolina)*. Charleston, SC: A.E. Miller, 1823.

Godbold, E. Stanly, and Robert H. Woody. *Christopher Gadsden and the American Revolution*. Knoxville: University of Tennessee Press, 1982.

Greenberg, Kenneth S. *Honor & Slavery: Lies, Duels, Noses, Masks, Dressing as a Woman, Gifts, Strangers, Humanitarianism, Death, Slave Rebellions, the Proslavery*

Argument, Baseball, Hunting, and Gambling in the Old South. Princeton, NJ: Princeton University Press, 1996.

Greene, Nathanael. *The Papers of General Nathanael Greene*. Edited by Richard K. Showman and Dennis Michael Conrad. Chapel Hill: University of North Carolina Press, 1976.

Greener, W.W. *The Gun and Its Development*. 9th ed. New York: Bonanza Books, 1967.

Gregg, Alexander, and John Julius Dargan. *History of the Old Cheraws; Containing an Account of the Aborigines of the Pedee, the First White Settlements, Their Subsequent Progress, Civil Changes, the Struggle of the Revolution, and Growth of the Country Afterward…* Salem, MA: Reprint Co., 1965.

Hamilton, Joseph. *The Only Approved Guide through All the Stages of a Quarrel: Containing the Royal Code of Honor*. London: Hatchard & Sons, 1829.

Hartwell, Edward Mussey. "The Study of Anatomy, Historically and Legally Considered." *Journal of Social Science* 11 (1880): 54–88.

Hatley, M. Thomas. *The Dividing Paths: Cherokees and South Carolinians through the era of Revolution*. London: Oxford Univeristy Press, 1993.

Historical Manuscripts Division. *The Manuscripts of the Earl of Dartmouth: American Papers*. Vol. II. London: Eyre and Spottiswoode for Her Majesty's Stationary Office, 1895.

Hogg, Ian V. *The Complete Handgun: 1300 to Present*. New York: Exeter Books, 1979.

Holland, Barbara. *Gentlemen's Blood: A History of Dueling from Swords at Dawn to Pistols at Dusk*. New York: Bloomsbury, 2003.

Hooper, George W., and John Lyde Wilson. *Down the River, or Practical Lessons under the Code Duello*. New York: E.J. Hale, 1874.

Hopkins, Andrea. *Tournaments and Joust: Training for War in Medieval Times*. New York: Rosen Publishing Group, 2004.

Horres, C. Russell. "An Affair of Honor at Fort Sumter." *South Carolina Historical Magazine* 102, no. 1 (January 2001): 6–26.

Horton, Tom. "Remembering the Howe-Gadsden Duel of 1778." *Moultrie News*, April 29, 2009: 2.

Hussey, Jeanette M., and Frances Stevenson Wein. "The Code Duello in America: On Exhibition in the National Portrait Gallery." Washington, D.C.: Smithsonian Institution Press, December 18, 1980.

Isenberg, Nancy. *Fallen Founder: The Life of Aaron Burr*. New York: Viking, 2007.

Johnson, Judy J. *What's So Wrong with Being Right? The Dangerous Nature of Dogmatic Belief*. New York: Prometheus Books, 2008.

Jones, Mark R. *Wicked Charleston*. Charleston, SC: The History Press, 2006.

Kaeuper, Richard. *Chivalry and Violence in Medieval Europe*. London: Oxford University Press, 1999.

Kane, Harnett T., Ralph Ray and Carl H. Pforzheimer. *Gentlemen, Swords and Pistols*. New York: Morrow, 1951.

Kellett, Rachel E. "Single Combat and Warfare in German Literature of the High Middle Ages: Stricker's 'Karl der Grosse' and 'Daniel von dem Blul henden Tal.'" PhD thesis, London, Maney Publishing for the Modern Humanities Resaearch Association, 2008.

Kentucky Secretary of State—Home. www.sos.ky.gov.

King, William L. *The Newspaper Press of Charleston, SC: A Chronological and Biographical History, Embracing a Period of One Hundred and Forty Years*. Charleston, SC: E. Perry, 1872.

Koerner, Brenden. "Demanding Satisfaction, to a Young Nation's Detriment." August 20, 2010. www.microkhan.com.

Kurtzman, Dr. Howard, clinical psychiatrist, interview by Grahame Long. September 8, 2011.

LaCroix, Alison L. "To Gain the Whole World and Lose His Own Soul: Noneteenth-Century American Dueling as Public Law and Private Code." *Hofstra Law Review* 33, no. 501 (2005): 501–69.

Ladd, Joseph Brown, Elizabeth Ladd Haskins and W.B. Chittenden. *The Literary Remains of Joseph Brown Ladd, M.D.* New York: H.C. Sleight, 1832.

"Letters, Notes, and Correspondences Concerning Dueling in Charleston." Charleston, SC: (SCCR 4571) Charleston Museum Archives.

Lindsay, Merrill. "Pistols Shed Light on Famed Duel." *Smithsonian Magazine* (November 1976): 94–97.

Lovell, Caroline Couper. *The Golden Isles of Georgia.* Los Angeles: Little, Brown and Co., 1932.

Lynn, John A. *Giant of the Grand Siècle: The French Army, 1610–1715.* Cambridge: Cambridge University Press, 1997.

Magruder, Harriet. *A History of Louisiana.* Boston: D.C. Heath & Co., 1909.

Massey, Gregory D. *John Laurens and the American Revolution.* Columbia: University of South Carolina Press, 2000.

Matheny, Paul, chief curator of art, South Carolina State Museum, interview by Grahame Long. October 26, 2011.

Moore, John Hammond. *Carnival of Blood: Dueling, Lynching, and Murder in South Carolina, 1880–1920.* Columbia: University of South Carolina Press, 2006.

Moore, Stephen West. "Letters of Stephen West Moore, 1823." Charleston, SC: Charleston Museum Archives.

Moultrie, William. *Memoirs of the American Revolution So Far As It Related to the States of North and South Carolina, and Georgia.* Vol. II. New York: David Longworth, 1802.

Murray-Flutter, Mark, senior curator of arms, Royal Armouries, interview by Grahame Long. August 23, 2003.

Neilson, George. *Trial by Combat*. Glasgow, Scotland: W. Hodge, 1890.

New York Times. "The Cash-Shannon Duel: A Cold-Blooded Murder on the 'Field of Honor.'" July 11, 1880. www.nytimes.com/ref/membercenter/nytarchive.html.

"Papers Touching Interview of April 23, 1862." Charleston, SC: (1975.125) Charleston Museum Archives.

Paullin, Charles Oscar. "Dueling in the Old Navy." *United States Naval Institute Proceedings* 35, no. 4 (1909): 1156–197.

Petigru, James L., and James Petigru Carson. *Life, Letters and Speeches of James Louis Petigru, the Union Man of South Carolina*. Washington, D.C.: W.H. Lowdermilk & Co., 1920.

Pollard, H.B.C. *A History of Firearms*. London: Butler & Tanner, Ltd., 1926.

Powell, George A. *Duelling Stories of the Sixteenth Century…* London: A.H. Bullen, 1904.

Prioleau, Charles Kuhn. "Correspondence to George Trenholm, 1860–1865." Charleston: (1280.00) South Carolina Historical Society.

Quincy, Josiah. *Memoir of the Life of John Quincy Adams*. Boston: Phillips, Sampson and Co., 1858.

———. *Memoir of the Life of Josiah Quincy Jun. of Massachusetts*. Boston: Cummings, Hilliard, & Company, 1825.

Ramsay, David. *A History of South-Carolina: From Its First Settlement in 1670, to the Year 1808*. Newberry, SC: W.J. Duffie, 1858.

Rauschenberg, Bradford L., and John Bivens. *The Furniture of Charleston, 1680–1820*. Vol. I. Winston-Salem, NC: Old Salem, Inc., 2003.

Ravenel, Harriott Horry. *Charleston, the Place and the People*. New York: Macmillan Co., 1906.

Reed, Jospeh J. "The Satisfaction Usual Among Gentlemen." *Lippincott's Magazine of Literature, Science and Education* (1869): 533–39.

Robertson, William. *The Works of William Robertson, D.D.: To Which Is Prefixed an Account of the Life and Writings of the Author by Dugald Stewart; in eight volumes.* Edinburgh, Scotland: Walker and Grieg, 1818.

Rogers, George C. "The Papers of James Grant of Ballindalloch Castle, Scotland." *South Carolina Historical Magazine* 77 (February 1976): 146–48.

Roman, Alfred. *The Military Operations of General Beauregard in the War Between the States, 1861–1865: Including a Brief Personal Sketch and Narrative of His Services in the War with Mexico.* New York: Harper & Brothers, 1884.

Rotton, J., and E.G. Cohn. "Outdoor Temperature, Climate Control and Criminal Assault: The Spatial and Temporal Ecology of Violence." *Environment and Behavior* 36, no. 2 (2004): 276–306.

Rowe, Charles R. *Pages of History: 200 Years of the Post and Courier.* Charleston, SC: Evening Post Publishing Co., 2003.

Rowland, Lawrence Sanders, Alexander Moore and George C. Rogers. *A History of Beaufort County, South Carolina.* Columbia: University of South Carolina Press, 1996.

Russell, William. *The History of Modern Europe with an Account of the Decline and Fall of the Roman Empire, and a View of the Progress of Society from the Rise of the Modern Kingdoms to the Peace of Paris in 1763, in a Series of Letters from a Nobleman to His Son.* Philadelphia: H. Maxwell for William Birch and Abraham Small, 1800–1801.

Sabine, Lorenzo. *Biographical Sketches of Loyalists of the American Revolution, with an Historical Essay.* Boston: Little, Brown & Co., 1864.

———. *Notes on Duels and Duelling Alphabetically Arranged, with a Preliminary Historical Essay.* Boston: Crosby, Nichols & Co., 1855.

Sala, Adriano. *Pistols: History, Technology, and Models from 1550 to 1913.* Mechanicsburg, PA: Stackpole Books, 2005.

Shakespeare, William. *The Tragedy of Troilus and Cressida*. Revised. New Haven, CT: Yale University Press, 1956.

Shakespeare, William, and John F. Andrews. *Antony and Cleopatra*. London: J.M. Dent, 1993.

Shoemaker, Robert B. "The Taming of the Duel: Masculinity, Honour and Ritual Violence in London, 1660–1800." *Historical Journal* 45, no. 3 (2002): 252–545.

Simms, William Gilmore. *The History of South Carolina from Its First European Discovery to Its Erection into a Republic*. New York: Redfield, 1860.

Sims, James Marion, and Harry Marion-Sims. *The Story of My Life*. New York: D. Appleton and Company, 1838.

South Carolina Historical and Genealogical Magazine 258.

South Carolina Legislature—Code of Laws. January 17, 2012. www.scstatehouse.gov.

Stevens, William Oliver. *Pistols at Ten Paces: The Story of the Code of Honor in America*. Boston: Mifflin & Co., 1940.

Steward, Dick. *Duels and the Roots of Violence in Missouri*. Columbia: University of Missouri Press, 2000.

Taylor, Rosser Howard. *Ante-bellum South Carolina: A Social and Cultural History*. Chapel Hill: University of North Carolina Press, 1942.

Tinkler, Robert. *James Hamilton of South Carolina*. Baton Rouge: Louisiana State University Press, 2004.

Tocqueville, Alexis de. *Democracy in America*. Vol. II. London: Saunders and Otley, 1835.

Trimpi, Helen P. *Crimson Confederates: Harvard Men Who Fought for the South*. Knoxville: University of Tennessee Press, 2010.

Truman, Benjamin Cummings. *The Field of Honor: Being a Complete and Comprehensive History of Duelling in All Countries; Including the Judicial Duel of Europe, the Private Duel of the Civilized World, and Specific Descriptions of All the Noted Hostile Meetings in Europe and America*. New York: Fords, Howard, & Hulbert, 1884.

Twain, Mark. *Europe and Elsewhere*. New York: Harper and Bros., 1929.

Twain, Mark, Harriet Elinor Smith and Benjamin Griffin. *Autobiography of Mark Twain*. Berkeley: University of California Press, 2010.

United States War Department. *The 1863 Laws of War: Articles of War General Orders No. 100 Army Regulations*. Mechanicsburg, PA: Stackpole Books, 2005.

Vanderhorst, Arnoldus. "Arnoldus Vanderhorst Dueling Papers, 1862–1868." Charleston: (1169.02.07) South Carolina Historical Society.

Wallace, David Duncan. *The Life of Henry Laurens*. New York: Knickerbocker Press, 1915.

Wallace, Kelly. "W.H. Rejects Bush-Saddam Duel Offer." CNN World, articles.cnn.com/2002-10-03/world/iraq.bush.duel. October 3, 2002.

Waring, Joseph Ioor. "Medicine in Charleston 1750–1775." *Annals of Medical History* 7, no. 1 (1935): 19–26.

Watson, Charles S. *The History of Southern Drama*. Lexington: University Press of Kentucky, 1997.

Weems, Mason L. *God's Revenge Against Duelling, or, The Duellists Looking Glass: Exhibiting That Gentlemanly Mode of Turning the Corner, in Features Altogether Novel and Admirably Calculated to Entertain and Instruct American Youth*. Georgetown, SC: Elijah Weems, 1820.

———. *A History of the Life and Death, Virtues and Exploits of General George Washington*. Philadelphia: John Bioren, n.d.

Whaley, Edward Mitchell. "Short Account of the Experiences of Edward Mitchell Whaley of Edisto Island, S.C., 1909." Charleston: (43/474) South Carolina Historical Society.

Williams, Jack K. *Dueling in the Old South: Vignettes in Social History*. College Station: Texas A&M University Press, 1980.

Wilson, John Lyde. *The Code of Honor; or Rules for the Governernment of Principals and Seconds in Duelling*. Charleston, SC: Thomas J. Eccles, 1838.

Wise, Stephen R. *Gate of Hell: Campaign for Charleston Harbor, 1863*. Columbia: University of South Carolina Press, 1994.

Wright, Cantey. *Edisto: A Guide to Life on the Island*. Charleston, SC: The History Press, 2006.

Yates, William Black. "Reminiscenses, 1867–1871." Charleston: (43/348) South Carolina Historical Society.

Zacks, Richard. *An Underground Education*. New York: Anchor Books, 1997.

INDEX

Twentieth South Carolina
    Volunteer Infantry 85

U

United States Navy 22
University of South Carolina. *See* South Carolina College
U.S. War Department 104

V

Vader, Darth 23
Vanderhorst, Arnoldus 105, 106
Vaux Hall Garden 65
Vendue Range 21
vengeance 16, 77
Victorian period 31, 65
Virginia 85

W

Wadboo Barony 24
Wadboo Creek 24
Waddell, James J. 22
wager of battle 25, 26, 27, 29, 99
Wagner, Thomas 105
Walker, Lucien M. 104
Wall, Gabriel 41
Waring, Archibald H. 22
Waring, M.N. 57
War of 1812 84
Washington, D.C. 103
Washington, George 20, 90, 92, 94, 100
Washington Race Course 41
Watchman and Southron 97
Weems, Mason Locke 100
West End Cemetery 86
West Point 104, 105
Whigs 78
White, John Blake 111

Wigfall, Louis T. 36
Wilderness, Battle of the 114
Wilson, John Lyde 47, 49, 50, 51, 55, 56, 57, 58, 60, 62, 69, 70, 73, 79, 81, 83, 85, 103, 112, 120
Wood, Richard 47

About the Author

J. Grahame Long is the curator of history at the Charleston Museum and has worked in various areas of Charleston history since graduating from Presbyterian College in 1996. He has published articles for various periodicals, including *Antiques and Fine Art*, *Silver Magazine*, *Charleston Magazine* and the *Charleston Mercury*, among others, and has worked as a historical analyst for A&E Networks, CNN and NPR. A native of Charlotte, North Carolina, Long is married to Lissa Long and has two daughters. He and his family split their time between Charleston and Edisto Island.

Visit us at
www.historypress.net